What's Ahead for American Business

What's Ahead for American Business

by

SUMNER H. Huber SLICHTER

An Atlantic Monthly Press Book

Little, Brown and Company · Boston

1951

Published April 1951
Reprinted April 1951
Reprinted October 1951

ATLANTIC—LITTLE, BROWN BOOKS
ARE PUBLISHED BY
LITTLE, BROWN AND COMPANY
IN ASSOCIATION WITH
THE ATLANTIC MONTHLY PRESS

Published simultaneously
in Canada by McClelland and Stewart Limited

PRINTED IN THE UNITED STATES OF AMERICA

Acknowledgments

THE MATERIAL in all of these chapters, except the second one, was presented in July, 1950, as a series of five lectures at the Ninth Business Conference of the Graduate School of Business at Stanford University. In revising the lectures for publication, I have somewhat expanded the material, but the substance is the same as I presented at Stanford. The essential parts of Chapters VI and VII were presented as one lecture.

The purpose of the Stanford lectures was to explore long-run trends. The rapid shift of the United States to a defense economy has made it seem desirable to add a discussion of short-run developments and their probable lasting effects upon the economy. This has been done in Chapter II, which was not presented at Stanford.

The interest of Dean Jackson of the Stanford Graduate School of Business in this attempt to see what is happening to the economy has been a source of encouragement. The manuscript has benefited greatly by the thorough and incisive criticism of Mr. Edward Weeks, Editor of the *Atlantic Monthly,* and by that of my wife.

S. H. S.

Contents

What's Ahead for American Business

CHAPTER I
The American Economy
before Korea

WHAT LONG-RUN INFLUENCES are molding the economy of the United States and what will it be like a generation or more hence? As everyone knows, it has been changing rapidly — it begins the second half of the new century as an economy very different from the one before the Great Depression and very different again from the one before the Second World War. New types of enterprises have grown up; methods of doing business have changed; the government plays a far greater role in the economy than it did fifty or even twenty years ago; trade unions, which were weak twenty years ago, have acquired great power; production has risen far faster than anyone would have dared hope in 1900; at the same time, the public debt and taxes have climbed to levels that would have terrified people in 1900 or 1929. Certainly the changes of the last fifty years have been far greater than people expected them to be, greater than the boldest forecaster would have dared to predict; furthermore, they show no signs of stopping. Consequently, one may be sure that the economy in thirty or fifty years will be very different from what it is today.

In the survey which follows I shall try to show what is happening to the American economy, and what are its prospects.

Will the standard of living continue to rise? Will government expenditures and taxes accelerate faster than production? What is likely to be the trend of prices? Will business be less subject to booms and depressions than it has been? How will the great power of trade unions affect their policies and their behavior? Is the economy capable of growing fast enough to provide jobs for the increasing labor force?

Finally, is the *basic* nature of the economy changing? Is private enterprise on the way out? Is the government going to dominate economic activities more and more completely, determining what people pay for goods, how large enterprises are permitted to be, how enterprises are run, how incomes are distributed? In short, is some sort of planned economy or welfare state gradually displacing capitalism?

Many of these questions about economic trends have been given added force by the Korean war. The conflict is unquestionably speeding up certain developments; for example, it is forcing the government to increase its expenditures substantially, to raise taxes, and to extend its controls over economic activities; it may also bring about developments which might otherwise have been escaped.

My examination of the prospects will be divided into seven principal parts.

To begin with, I wish to examine the most important changes that have occurred in the past several decades. This is a good way to gain light on existing and probable future trends. In the second place, I wish to inquire into the lasting effects of our present defense economy. Third, I wish to analyze some of the prospective changes and trends that, even before the Korean war, seemed likely to occur, and that still must be expected. Fourth, I wish to explore some of those areas where the future characteristics of the economy are very much in doubt. In the fifth place, I wish to examine our position in the world economy. Sixth, I wish to investigate the much-disputed capacity of the economy to grow. Finally, I wish to analyze such questions as whether the United States is going socialist or whether it is likely to develop some form of planned economy. Since the course of history is largely guided by ideas, part of my analysis will be an exploration of the ideas that are likely to mold history in the near future.

The changes of the last several decades fall into three principal groups: changes in institutions and business practices; changes in economic conditions; and changes in ideas about the economy and how it should operate.

CHANGES IN INSTITUTIONS AND BUSINESS PRACTICES

In the last fifty years economic institutions and business practices have changed rapidly — the monetary system has virtually been revolutionized; business practices have been modified by the rise of the staff in business organizations and by such developments as intention-to-spend reports, the term loan, and super venture-capital companies; most important of all, the growth of trade unions has introduced a new economic power into the community and the extension of the economic activities of the government has modified the method of making many decisions. Let us examine briefly some of these changes in economic institutions.

Revolutionary changes in the monetary system. Until 1933, the principal way in which money came into existence was through short-term borrowing by business concerns. In 1929, the loans of commercial banks accounted for nearly two thirds of the country's supply of money. This was an unsatisfactory state of affairs because it made our economy unduly sensitive to unfavorable developments and liable to severe contraction. When banks became pessimistic or doubtful about the immediate future of business, they reduced their lending. This forced borrowers to use part of their income to pay off their debts. Since the banks were not creating money to make new loans as fast as the old loans were being paid off, the money supply of the country was contracted and the recession in business was made worse. How serious a large contraction in short-term loans can be is indicated by the fact that in 1929 the outstanding loans of commercial banks were about 38 per cent as large as the net national product for the year.

The large-scale borrowing by the government during the great depression and the Second World War shifted the principal source of the money supply. At the end of 1950, short-term private bank loans (mainly to business concerns) accounted for less than one third of the money supply and about 57 per cent of the demand deposits. These loans are less than one fifth of the annual net national product of the United States. The largest single source of money supply is borrowing by the government. The holdings of government obligations by commercial banks are substantially larger than their short-term loans. A contraction in business does not cause the banks to insist that the government pay off part of its debt to them. Consequently, a drop in business today has much less tendency to bring about a reduction in the money supply.

The rise of staff in business organizations. Prior to 1900, there were few staff jobs in business — managements consisted almost entirely of line officers who made their decisions as best they could with little advance investigation of problems by staff departments and without the help of recommendations on policies by the staff. But change came with bigness. For example, credit departments in banks were virtually unknown until after 1900. Today every large bank has a credit department. Most large and medium-sized concerns today have divisions of marketing, product development, accounting, and industrial relations. These staffs assist line officers in handling current operations, in developing new policies, and in making plans for the future. Much of the success of management in raising the productivity of labor is attributable to the growth of staff work. Most spectacular and important of all staff developments has been the rise of technological research. Expenditures on industrial research were small at the beginning of the century. Now they are many times larger than the expenditures of all of the universities of the country.

The development of intention-to-spend reports. One of the most important and interesting recent improvements in our economy has been the publication of information about intentions — intentions of farmers to plant, intentions of business enterprises to spend on equipment, and intentions of consumers to buy various classes of goods, particularly automobiles, refrigerators, washing machines, and houses. Until very recently business managers and government officials have been forced to make decisions about future trends by examining recent ones and judging whether or not they would continue. The collection of representative information about intentions now for the first time enables business concerns and government agencies to make plans on the basis of more or less direct information about the future behavior of our economy.

The intention-to-spend reports have not always turned out to be accurate, and it must not be expected that they always will be. Every now and then unforeseen developments may cause sudden changes in plans to spend. Had intention-to-spend reports been collected in the middle of 1929, for example, they would undoubtedly have been very different from the actual amount of spending after the stock market crash in October. One of the purposes of the intention-to-spend reports, of course, is to induce actions by the government or business that change the willingness to spend. For example, intentions to spend too much may induce stricter credit controls, and intentions to cut spending may cause business concerns or the government to encourage spending. Indeed, the intention-to-spend reports may be most useful when they induce action that causes them not to be true!

The rise of the term loan. It has always been true that many so-called "short-term" loans of banks have been renewed several times and were made with the expectation on the part of both sides that there would be renewals. Consequently, many so-called short-term loans were not really short-term at all. During the last twenty years, however, commercial banks have developed a new type of loan known as the "term loan." These loans may run up to five years or more, with a part of the total amount maturing each year. Thus if 500,000 dollars is the total amount lent, one fifth, or 100,000 dollars, may mature each year.

This new type of loan is particularly useful to enterprises which are expanding and which need to raise capital more quickly and simply than can be done by selling a bond issue to the public. Also the money which is lent when a commercial bank makes a term loan is created by the bank and thus helps to increase the money supply.[1] The country needs to have its supply of money grow as the output of goods rises in order that an increasing demand for goods may accompany the expansion of production. Until 1933, as I have said, the principal way in which the money supply was expanded was through the making of short-term loans by commercial banks. I have pointed out that this way of getting money created had its drawbacks, and that between 1933 and 1945 most of the money supply came into existence by the government's borrowing from banks. But it would be undesirable for the country to be too dependent upon a rise in the public debt for an increase in its money supply — because that would require that the public debt be quite large in relation to output and

[1] Insurance companies also make term loans but they do not create money — they lend part of the premium payments made to them.

incomes. The term loan offers a way of increasing the money supply that is much superior to the short-term commercial loan. Since term loans mature gradually, over a period of years, their repayment is less likely to aggravate a contraction in business than is the repayment of an equal volume of short-term loans.

The development of super venture-capital enterprises. The community has never had regular and organized ways of putting capital into new enterprises. The success of new concerns in obtaining capital has depended upon the ability of the originators to supply it from their own resources or the resources of relatives and friends, or upon their ability to convince well-to-do persons that the project offers a good opportunity for investment. The prospective investors have usually been unprepared to make adequate investigations of new projects.

The need for thorough investigation of investment opportunities is particularly great when the concern is a new one. The need is double if the venture involves bringing out a new product, using new methods of production, operating under new conditions, or entering new markets. In addition, it is desirable that some of the investors in new enterprises be prepared to supply managerial advice. Finally, it is desirable that the investors be prepared to put in more than the planned amount, in case the concern requires more capital than was originally estimated — as often happens. Difficulties in getting a new process to work, or in creating a demand for a new product, may make the survival of a new concern dependent upon its ability to obtain additional capital.

Now that stiff progressive income taxes are encroaching heavily upon the large incomes in the community, new and better ways are needed for getting capital into enterprises. Consequently, the super venture-capital companies that have recently come into existence mark an important step forward in our economy. They are staffed to investigate the kind of investment opportunities that are difficult to appraise; they are prepared to offer managerial advice; they are prepared to put in additional capital if that seems necessary and worth while; they offer the small investor or the man of moderate means an opportunity to invest a small amount of capital in a variety of new ventures. It remains to be seen whether the new venture-capital companies can make a profit out of economic pioneering. They are bound to make mistakes, and the losses from a few mistakes will offset the gains from a number of successful ventures. There can be little doubt, however, that the least wasteful way to supply capital for new enterprises is through concerns that specialize in doing this very thing.

The rise of chain stores and mail-order houses. Chain stores and mail-order houses have been in the main a development of the last fifty years. One of their most important aspects is that they offer to new manufacturers ready-made and cheap nation-wide distribution facilities. In a nation as large as the United States, the cost of marketing a new article may be the chief obstacle to introducing it. The availability of marketing outlets that can reach millions of consumers promptly and at low mark-ups makes it easier for new manufacturers to start in business.

Chain stores and mail-order houses also improve our

economy by making it more competitive. They do this partly by encouraging competition among suppliers and partly by their policy of avoiding the accumulation of slow-moving items. By cutting prices they get rid of goods that do not sell readily. Finally, chain stores and mail-order houses make prices more responsive to changes in demand. In periods of contracting demand, manufacturers are loath to cut prices because they have no assurance that price reductions will be passed on to consumers. Hence, the manufacturer reasons that price cuts will do little good in stimulating sales. Mail-order houses and chain stores, however, are in a position to initiate price cuts to consumers and to find manufacturers who will supply goods at prices consistent with the reductions. Thanks to these institutions, therefore, our economy is much better equipped than ever before to gets its prices adjusted to changes in demand.

The rise of trade unions. Next to the growing intervention of the government in economic matters, the most important change in the economy has been the growth in the power of trade unions. As late as 1929, less than 10 per cent of non-executive and nontechnical employees were union members. Today, the trade union membership is about four times as large as in 1929. About two thirds of the nonexecutive and nontechnical workers in manufacturing, four fifths of such workers in mining, four fifths in construction, and four fifths in transportation are members of trade unions.

Trade unions represent the strongest organizations of sellers in the country and some of the unions — such as the United Steel Workers, which is able to deprive the country of steel, or the United Mine Workers, which is able to deprive the country of coal, or several of the operating rail-road unions, which are able to deprive the country of rail-road service — are undoubtedly the most powerful economic organizations the country has ever possessed.

Trade unions have possessed great power too short a time for their effects upon our economy to be pronounced, but there is no doubt that unions will eventually have far-reaching effects. A few unions, such as that of the long-shoremen, have been able to limit substantially the output of their members, thereby tending to reduce the standard of living of the country. The strong pressure of unions for higher wages, however, has undoubtedly helped to raise the standard of living because this pressure has forced management to work harder to keep down labor costs and has thereby accelerated technological progress. Most unions are strong enough to push up wages of labor faster than managers and engineers can raise output per man-hour. As a result, the long-run movement of prices is likely to be upward. This will have far-reaching consequences because it will impose large losses on savers who have continued to put their money into savings accounts, bonds, life insurance, or annuities.

The growth of unions means that, more promptly and completely than ever, a rise in the demand for labor will cause employees to insist upon higher wages. The practical consequences will bear watching. If the growth of unions means that increases in the demand for labor will have a greater tendency to raise wages, then increases in the demand for labor may be less effective in producing more employment.

The rise in the importance of the government in the economy. The greatest single change in our economic institutions during the past half-century has been the expansion of the economic activities of the government. These activities are now extraordinarily pervasive and take a wide variety of forms. The government is steadily becoming a more and more important producer of goods and services and also a larger and larger consumer of goods; by means of taxes, subsidies, and various grants, the government greatly modifies the distribution of income; it regulates a growing number of prices, putting floors under some and ceilings over others; finally, it imposes an increasing number of rules that determine how economic activities must or must not be conducted.

The growing importance of the government as a producer is indicated by the fact that it now turns out about one tenth of the country's output of goods and services compared with about one seventeenth in 1929. The labor cost of the goods and services produced by the government in 1949 was 21.8 billion dollars.[2] The productive activities of

[2] In estimating the proportion of the country's output produced by the government and government enterprises, the figures for national income, not for the net national product, are used. The reason is that the contribution of the government to production is measured in terms of factor costs — since there is no market price for most of the goods provided by the government. Hence the factor cost of the goods provided by the government should be compared with the factor cost of the national product. The national income is the factor cost of the national product. As a matter of fact, the costs of production by the government are underestimated, since no allowance is made for the cost of capital used by the government or in government enterprises.

the government are manifold. In addition to the usual activities of providing security and maintaining order, the government is a large lender of money; it is in the housing business on a substantial scale; various government-owned plants produce about 20 per cent of the country's electricity; through provision of highways and airfields, the government provides much of the capital used in the transportation business; the government produces large quantities of statistics and other information that businessmen and farmers use in planning their operations and that trade unions and employers use in their negotiations.

The growing role of the government as a consumer is indicated by the fact that in 1950 it consumed over 42.1 billion dollars of goods and services, or 15 per cent of the net national product as compared with 9 per cent in 1929.[3] A part of the purchase of goods by the government is in the nature of an investment (roads, bridges, dams, water works, school buildings) and adds to the country's productive capacity. For example, in 1949, 6.4 billion dollars of the goods purchased by the government represented new construction. During the last twenty years the government's consumption of goods has grown over twice as fast as its production of goods.

The redistribution of income by the government is shown by the rapid rise of taxes on personal income, especially on high incomes, and by the great increase in payments based on need. Taxes rose from 2.6 billion dollars on total personal

[3] The figures do not include consumption of goods by government enterprises such as TVA, the Alaskan Railroad, and other government-owned industrial enterprises.

incomes of 85.1 billion in 1929 to 20.4 billion on incomes of 222.4 billion in 1950. As a result of the stiff progressive income tax, the total income after taxes of all persons receiving 25,000 dollars a year or more was one sixth less in 1948 than in 1928, although the *number* of persons receiving incomes of 25,000 dollars or more was almost 60 per cent greater in 1949 than in 1928.

The redistribution of income is carried further by large payments to persons in return for no services rendered — that is, on the basis of need. Between 1929 and 1949, such payments (pensions, unemployment compensation, old-age assistance, for example) increased over four times as fast as personal incomes — from 1.3 billion dollars, or 1.5 per cent of all personal incomes, to 12.6 billion dollars, or 6.1 per cent of all personal incomes.[4] An important effect of the large growth of payments based upon need is to make the level of personal incomes less dependent upon the level of production and employment. Today, a contraction of production and employment would have less effect upon incomes than ever before. For example, the rise in the average

---

[4] This estimate of payments of 12.6 billion dollars based upon need differs slightly from the estimate of "transfer payments" (payments not in return for productive services) made by the Department of Commerce for 1949, which was 12.3 billion. From the Department of Commerce estimate of transfer payments I have subtracted consumer bad debts (estimated by the Department at 258 million dollars) as these are hardly payments based on need. To the Department of Commerce estimates of transfer payments I have added compensation for injuries (estimated by the Department at 617 million dollars for 1949), classified by the Department as a supplement to wages and salaries.

amount of unemployment from 2.1 million in 1948 to 3.4 million in 1949 caused payments for unemployment compensation to rise more than a billion — from 818 million dollars in 1948 to 1837 million dollars in 1949. Thus the drop in personal incomes was limited.

The government regulates the prices of an increasing number of commodities. The community has been refusing more and more to accept the prices that free markets set and has insisted that the government put floors under some prices and ceilings over others. Examples of ceilings are railroad rates, electric light and power rates, gas rates, telephone rates; examples of floors are the minimum wage of 75 cents an hour imposed by the Federal government on most concerns engaged in interstate commerce, and the many floors applied to farm products. In the fiscal year 1949–1950, a year of good employment, the government spent about 1.4 billion dollars in keeping up the prices of agricultural products.

Finally, there has been a great expansion of the areas in which the government prescribes the rules of the game. During recent years the government has undertaken to provide rather detailed rules for the conduct of industrial relations. For example, when the appropriate unit for bargaining is in dispute, the government determines what it shall be. It enforces on each side the obligation to bargain, it requires employers and unions to give each other notice of their desire to negotiate changes in agreements, and it forbids many kinds of behavior known as "unfair labor practices."

The government also regulates capital markets in considerable detail. Security issues that are offered to the public must go through an elaborate procedure administered by the Securities and Exchange Commission. The government has been attempting to develop rules regulating pricing of commodities by business enterprises. But government officials do not seem to have a clear idea of what these rules should be or what purpose they should serve. For example, there is confusion as to whether government policy should aim to give consumers the benefit of stiff competition or to protect business concerns from too severe competition. The government does in a general way undertake to encourage competition, but it also discourages certain types of price cutting. Discriminatory price cutting is outlawed, but the line between reasonable classification of customers and unfair discrimination is far from clear. Of late years some government officials have been holding that success in capturing a large part of the market may cause a concern to be in violation of the law. Hence, an enterprise may violate the law (in the view of some government officials) either (1) because it competes too successfully or (2) because it imposes restraints on competition or joins with others to impose them.

CHANGES IN ECONOMIC CONDITIONS

Of the recent changes in economic conditions I have selected seven that seem to me to be particularly important.

The contest between the United States and Soviet Russia. The contest between the United States and Russia affects the operation of our economy in many ways. Even after the peak of defense expenditures has been passed, the United States will have to spend between 30 billion and 40 billion dollars a year on defense and foreign aid. This will be over 10 per cent of the national income and around 10 per cent of the net national product.[5] The conflict between the United States and Russia will cause the demand for goods to be greater and more insistent than in times of peace; it will stimulate research in basic science and technology; it will encourage the United States to develop trade with that part of the world outside the Russian sphere of influence; it will put the trade unions in an unusually strong bargaining position.

Whether the strong demand for goods and the absorption of a considerable part of the country's output will accelerate or retard the growth of our economy will depend in large

[5] Mr. Emanuel Shinwell, the British Minister of Defense, speaking before Parliament on July 26, 1950, estimated that the Soviet Union is spending at least 13 per cent of its national income on armaments. (*Economist,* July 29, 1950; Vol. CLIX, p. 202.) The *Economist* estimated that defense expenditures in 1949 or 1949–50 in the United Kingdom were 7.4 per cent of the national income; in France, 5.0 per cent; in Italy, 3.8 per cent; in Sweden, 3.6 per cent; in Canada, 3.0 per cent; in Belgium, 2.5 per cent; in Norway, 2.5 per cent. (*Ibid.,* p. 201.)

The national income is the compensation of the several factors of production used to turn out the national product. It consists of wages, interest, rent, profits, and the net income of the self-employed. The net national product is the output of the country at market prices — except the output of the government which is valued at cost. The difference between the national income and the national product is mainly represented by indirect business tax payments.

measure upon our public policies. Thus the long-run movement in the standard of living of the country depends more
than ever upon the government.

The accumulation of individual savings in recent years.
During the last ten years there has been an enormous increase in the volume of personal saving in the United States.
During this period individuals added about 175 billion
dollars to their savings — more than the amount they had
added during the previous thirty years. Of course, a large
proportion of the community has small or negligible holdings of such assets as cash, savings deposits, or government
bonds. Nevertheless, early in 1950, about 42 out of 100
spending units had savings accounts, and 39 out of 100
owned government savings bonds.[6]

The huge increase in savings was made possible by the
Second World War, which greatly increased incomes after
taxes but limited the expansion in the output of consumer
goods. In fact, the war compelled substantial reductions in
the output of some types of consumer goods, such as automobiles and durable household articles. Most of the increase
in personal savings during the war had to take the form
of an increase in liquid assets (cash, bank deposits, and

[6] *Federal Reserve Bulletin,* December 1950, p. 1594. A "spending unit" is defined as *all persons living in the same dwelling and
belonging to the same family who pool their income to meet their
major expenses.* Under this definition, the number of spending units
is greater than the number of families (since some members of the
same family who live in the same dwelling may not pool their income to meet major expenses) and smaller than the number of individual income receivers (since many spending units have more
than one income receiver).

government securities) because restrictions on civilian production during the war years caused decreases in the output of private industrial plant and equipment and of housing.

Unfortunately, most of the liquid assets accumulated during the last ten years have less purchasing power than in
the year in which they were made — because of the rise of
more than 70 per cent in the price level since 1940. For example, by the end of 1945, individuals had accumulated
about 85.4 billion dollars in the form of savings deposits,
savings and loan shares, and United States government
securities. Most of these savings that were in the possession
of individuals in December 1945 were undoubtedly in their
possession in December 1949 when personal holdings of
savings deposits, savings and loan shares, and United States
government securities, totaled 105.5 billion dollars.[7] Although the total dollar value of these three forms of personal
savings was greater at the end of 1949 than at the end of
1945, the purchasing power was down by about 4 per cent.
Individuals have fared much better in their investments in
homes.

The growth of home ownership. Ten years ago tenants
outnumbered owners. Today owners are more numerous
than tenants. Indeed, of the 23 million single-family nonfarm homes in the United States, about 20 million are occu-
pied by owners. In addition, about 1.5 million out of
5,250,000 two-family dwellings have owner-occupants. The
tremendous rise in home ownership is largely attributable

[7] The figures do not include that part of personal savings represented by trust funds.

to ceilings on rents, which led to a drop in the construction of houses for rent. Nearly all of the single-family houses built in the last five years have been sold to owner-occupiers and most of the houses vacant in 1940 have also been sold to owner-occupiers.

The decrease in private debt relative to the net national product. The depression and the Second World War have brought about a drop in private debt relative to the national product. During the depression there was an actual decrease in the volume of private debt — partly because of defaults and partly because repayments were high in relation to new loans. During the war period, private debt grew slowly while the net national product, expressed in dollar terms, expanded rapidly. Since the end of the Second World War, private debt has been increasing faster than the net national product, but the debt is still small in relation to production. In 1949 the net national product was 2.8 times as large as in 1939, but the net private debt has increased only about 65 per cent above 1939.[8]

The increase in the public debt. The net public debt of

[8] The changes in the net national product and private debt were as follows:

	Net national product	Total private debt	Corporate debt	Individual and noncorporate private debt
		(billions)		
1929	$ 95.0	$161.5	$ 88.9	$72.6
1939	83.2	125.5	73.5	52.0
1945	202.8	140.7	85.3	55.4
1949	236.8	205.5	111.6	93.8

the United States (states, localities, and the Federal government) was nearly eight times as large in 1948 as in 1929 and nearly four times as large as in 1939.[9] The public debt can undoubtedly become too large, but the growth of the public debt up to the present amount has added to the economic strength of the community. For example, the policy of financing part of the cost of the war by borrowing has made possible the increase in saving by individuals, unincorporated enterprises, and corporations. At the end of 1949, more than 41 billion dollars of the obligations of the Federal government were owned by individuals, nearly 22 billion dollars by trust funds, and about 54 billion dollars by nonbank corporations and unincorporated businesses. These government securities, though increasing the burden on taxpayers, greatly improve the financial position of the individuals and the businesses that own them.

The increase in the liquidity of the economy. By the "liquidity of the economy" is meant the volume of liquid assets (cash, bank deposits, and close equivalents to cash, such as government securities) in comparison with production, incomes, or other assets. There are three principal ways of measuring the liquidity of the economy. One is the volume of liquid assets in relation to the size of the net national product; a second is their volume in relation to the size of personal incomes; a third is their volume in relation to the amount of net private debts.

The growth in liquidity is attributable to the government

[9] *Survey of Current Business,* October 1949, p. 8. The public debt was 29.7 billion dollars in 1929, 58.9 billion in 1939, and 232.7 billion in 1948.

deficits during the depression and particularly during the war. These deficits led to a rapid growth in the money supply and in the holdings of government securities by individuals and business concerns. For example, total private domestic deposits and currency outside of banks increased from 63.3 billion dollars at the end of 1939 to about 150.8 billion dollars at the end of 1945, and the net debt of the Federal government, including guaranteed obligations outstanding, increased from about 41 billion dollars at the end of 1939 to about 252 billion dollars at the end of 1945.

It is of interest to note how great has been the rise in the liquidity of the economy. Between 1939 and 1949, the rise in the liquid assets of individuals and business, it is true, was not large relative to the net national product. There was, however, a considerable growth in the liquid asset holdings of individuals relative to personal incomes after taxes. In 1949 personal incomes after taxes were 2.7 times as large as in 1939, but the liquid assets of individuals were 3.6 times as large.[10] Equally noteworthy has been the rise of liquid assets of individuals and unincorporated businesses relative to individual and noncorporate debt. At the end of 1949 the debt was half as large relative to liquid assets as in 1939. Private debt has increased rapidly in the last several

[10] The following was the relationship between liquid asset holdings of individuals and personal incomes after taxes:

	Liquid asset holdings of individuals	Personal incomes after taxes
	(billions)	
1939	$ 49.6	$ 70.2
1949	177.0	187.4

years, but debts are still low relative to liquid assets.[11]

The great growth in holdings of liquid assets by individuals and enterprises has strengthened the economy because it gives both individuals and enterprises a sense of security and thus enhances their willingness to spend their current incomes on goods. But the liquidity of the economy also creates problems. For example, in 1950 and 1951, the huge holdings of liquid assets have complicated the problem of controlling inflation.

A great shift of power in the community represented by a drop in the prestige and influence of businessmen and a rise in the influence of the representatives of employees. During most of the history of the United States, the businessmen have been dominant but during the last twenty years there has been a sharp drop in the influence of businessmen, except farmers, and a rapid rise in the influence of trade unions. The shift in power is reflected in such policies as protection of the right of workers to organize, social security legislation, and the fair labor standards act. The abuse of their power by trade unions has caused some loss in the influence of employees (or at least unionized employees) since 1946 but it still remains true that the A.F. of L. and

[11] The relationship between the liquid assets of individuals and their debts was as follows:

	Liquid assets of individuals and unincorporated businesses	Individual and noncorporate debt
	(billions)	
1939	$ 56.0	$52.0
1949	200.8	93.8

the C.I.O. each have more weight in Washington than
the National Association of Manufacturers or the United
States Chamber of Commerce. Even the Taft-Hartley Act,
passed in the face of strenuous opposition of trade union
leaders, does not in reality impair the power of unions.
As a matter of fact, in so far as the law discourages abuses
in the activities of unions it probably strengthens unions
— though this was not the purpose of the law.

The drop in the influence of businessmen has been
brought about fundamentally by changes in the compo-
sition of the country's labor force and in the organization
and control of American industry. A hundred and fifty
years ago industry in the United States consisted mainly of
small owner-operated enterprises and the number of self-
employed persons was greater than the number of employees. Today, three fourths of the labor force consists of
wage earners, clerical workers, and other nonexecutive employees and one fourth consists of proprietors of owner-
operated businesses (including farms), managers, and professional or semiprofessional workers. Today corporations
produce half of the total output of the country and nearly
three fifths of the privately produced output. Corporations,
however, are not widely owned. Accurate information on
the ownership of corporations is lacking, but the total number of stockholders is apparently about 6 million — less than
one out of sixteen adults.[12] Few farmers or wage earners
are owners of corporate stock. The great majority of stockholders are corporate executives, owners of unincorporated

[12] About 8 times as many persons own automobiles as own stock
in corporations. (*Federal Reserve Bulletin,* December 1950, p. 1590.)

enterprises outside of agriculture, and professional men —
and the wives and widows of these people. Relatively few
stockholders are men of means whose principal income
is derived from property.

When about half of the gainfully employed persons in
the country owned and operated their own enterprises and
a large part of the employees looked forward to becoming
business owners, the dominant point of view of the community was sympathetic to business and the problems of
employees received little attention. Not until the third quarter of the nineteenth century, for example, did labor legislation begin to appear. In 1874 Massachusetts passed the first
enforceable law limiting the hours of work of women. As
the proportion of employees in the labor force gradually
increased and as corporations failed to become broadly
owned, the influence of businessmen on public policies
slowly declined. Following the turn of the century considerable labor legislation was passed — nearly all of it strongly
opposed by employers. Some of the legislation, such as the
New York law limiting the hours of work in bakeries, the
first minimum wage law, and legislation designed to protect the right to organize, were thrown out by the courts,
which tended to reflect the views of the nineteenth century.

The great crash of 1929, however, was the immediate cause
of the large drop in the influence of businessmen — particularly the influence of corporate executives. The people
blamed business for the issuance of large quantities of securities in the twenties, especially securities of public utility
holding companies, that soon became worth a small fraction
of the prices at which they had been offered. The people also

blamed business for encouraging speculation that led them to buy large quantities of stocks and real estate at high prices with borrowed money. The disastrous crash also persuaded millions of people that businessmen were wrong in contending that our economy could be trusted to run itself and convinced them that it had to be regulated to keep it stable and to make the distribution of income more equitable. Most people were not clear as to what they desired the government to do, but they were insistent that it abandon the policy of "hands off."

Most businessmen, especially the executives of large corporations, opposed proposals that the government regulate economic activities. The conflict between their views and the prevailing views of the community weakened the confidence of the community in the businessmen, and diminished their influence on public policy. They found themselves opposing rather than leading the dominant trends of the time. And among businessmen it is the corporate executives, as I have pointed out, who have suffered the greatest loss of influence.

Although farmers are businessmen, they are an exception to the general rule, since they have not lost influence during the last two decades. As a matter of fact, they have always held more or less aloof from the rest of the business community and have often been at odds with corporate business on issues of economic policy. Farmers fought the railroads on the question of rate regulation and at various times in the past they have had serious differences with the processors of farm products, such as millers, packers, cigarette manufacturers. In the last two decades, spurred to assert themselves because of their losses in the great depression, the farmers have gained influence while the rest of the business community has lost it. Indeed, the opposition of the farmers to some of the policies of trade unions has been a principal check upon the power of unions.

The sharp decline in the influence of businessmen upon public policies has raised doubts concerning the willingness of an economy composed primarily of employees to encourage enterprise. A dynamic and enterprising economy requires (1) rapid progress in technology; (2) adventurous and imaginative businessmen who are willing to attempt to put the discoveries of technology to industrial use, especially to develop markets for new products; and (3) investors who are willing to back new and risky ventures — to take long chances in the hope of making big gains. One may be confident that technology will make rapid advances, but it remains to be seen whether a community more or less preoccupied with the problems of employees will furnish a congenial environment for bold and adventurous businessmen and investors who gamble for large stakes.

CHANGES IN IDEAS

Most important of all the changes that have affected our economy in late years are changes in ideas and preferences. The essential change in ideas may be put in one sentence: It is the abandonment of the view that the economy is self-regulating and that it is a mistake for the government to interfere with its operation. The traditional view of "hands off" has been replaced by the view that the economy needs to be regulated in many respects and that the government must assume some responsibility for regulating it.

When the twentieth century began, most people still believed that the economy in the main should be left to run itself. Certain exceptions to this general policy were admitted, but they were few and they were definitely regarded as exceptions. For example, it was a hard struggle during the first two decades of the century to get workmen's compensation laws passed. Efforts to regulate minimum wage rates in sweated industries were held unconstitutional by the courts, and payments to the unemployed, such as were in effect in Britain, were scornfully referred to as "the dole."

Slowly, but inexorably, opinion changed. The Interstate Commerce Commission was given real authority over railroad rates. (The abuses of rebating were primarily responsible for this.) The courts accepted the idea that the hours of labor for women in general might be regulated and the hours of men in certain industries, such as railroading and mining. Banking difficulties in 1908 helped bring about the establishment of the Federal Reserve System in 1913, and the collapse of prices after the First World War, stimulated Reserve authorities to develop some control over credit. It was the great collapse of 1929, however, as I have pointed out, and slow and incomplete recovery from it, that transformed the thinking of the American people about their economy. This great economic disaster caused most people in the United States to abandon the idea that the economy can be left to run itself except in this, that, or some other respect, and to accept the view that the whole needs to be regulated. In short, the collapse of 1929 produced a revolution in thinking about economic policies.

One hears many reasons why our economy needs to be regulated. In some fields competition is regarded as too stiff, and as taking forms that are regarded as unfair. In some fields our economy shows a tendency to develop monopolies that will exploit buyers unless prevented. The distribution of income is regarded as unfair by many people, and they think that the government ought to do something about that. Private industry alone is not regarded as capable of meeting certain needs, such as the need for income during unemployment or illness or the need for income after retirement. But there are two principal reasons why people accept the view that regulation is necessary: first, they know that our economy is subject to ups and downs in production and employment and they want these ups and downs to be kept small; and second, they remember the great depression and slow recovery, and are afraid that our economy cannot be counted upon to expand fast enough to absorb the constantly growing number of job seekers.

The changing attitude of the American people toward the economy promises to bring about important modifications in the economy itself. In the days when the "hands off" philosophy was dominant, incomes, prices, production, and employment were permitted to adjust themselves to one fixed value — namely, the value of the domestic currency in terms of the currencies of other countries. The new philosophy that the economy cannot be trusted to run itself accepts a new fixed point of adjustment. That new point is "full employment." The view is that production, prices, and incomes should be adjusted to full employment. No matter what happens to prices and incomes, full employment must be maintained — or at least actual employment must be kept as close to full employment as possible. Perhaps the community will sooner or later change its ideas on this point. It has not yet had a chance to learn the problems and costs of maintaining full employment — or to discover the conflicts between full employment and other desirable objectives, such as stable prices. After the community has had experience with these conflicts, it may decide that full employment must not *always* take precedence.

To summarize, the people of the United States at the mid-century find themselves living in a highly dynamic economy — an economy which has been changing rapidly and which, in all probability, will continue to change rapidly. It has shown great capacity to develop new kinds of institutions and new methods of doing business. And this capacity to make progress has been enhanced by two world wars.

At this very time, when our economy has attained unprecedented strength, our economic and political institutions and our philosophy of life are challenged by Russia. The ideological war in which the world is engaged is not new, but during most of the last seventy-five years this war has been conducted within countries rather than between countries. Only in the last generation have the champions of the Communistic philosophy gained control of governments and thus acquired geographical bases from which to operate. Now they are able to conduct the ideological war more effectively than ever before. In interpreting this ideological war, it is important to remember that Communism is more distinctive and radical as a political philosophy than as an economic one. Its challenge to American values in the field of politics is more basic than its challenge in the field of economics. The refusal of Communism to recognize the civil rights of individuals is far more important than the ideas of Communism about the ownership of industry.

Finally, the people of the United States, with their highly dynamic and extraordinarily strong economy, are much divided as to how their economy should be operated. Although there is now general acceptance of the idea that it is not self-regulating, a substantial minority still challenge this view. The majority that desire a more or less government-guided economy are not agreed as to what they wish. There are no blueprints of policy that command general acceptance.

The people do not know whether the government can satisfactorily discharge the enormous new responsibilities that they expect it to assume. Furthermore, they do not know how the new activities will affect the political institutions and the political life of their country. They do not know, for example, whether a government which undertakes the responsibility of regulating many aspects of economic activities will be torn apart and rendered ineffective by a multitude of pressure groups.

The second half of the twentieth century, therefore, like the first half, seems destined to be a period of rapid change in technology, in economic institutions, in economic policies, and possibly in political institutions.

CHAPTER II
The Long-run Implications
of the Defense Economy

THE SHIFT TO A DEFENSE ECONOMY

UNTIL THE OUTBREAK OF FIGHTING in Korea it had been expected that the United States could build up a sufficiently strong military establishment to deter attack without imposing a multitude of special controls upon the economy. The armed services were to have been increased gradually to about 3 millions and this increase and the provision of the necessary equipment was to have been spread over a period of four years. But the fighting with the North Koreans and the entry of the Chinese caused a speed-up in the rate of rearmament and the scale had to be substantially enlarged. The armed forces are expected to reach 3 million by the end of 1951 and the size may (temporarily at least) go well beyond 3 million. No figures on the amount of military equipment that will be needed have been issued and perhaps none can be provided, since needs change with development in the technology of war and with changes in international relations. The outlays on military equipment during the next several years, however, will be very large.

Such rapid increase in the armed forces and such huge outlays on military equipment have brought about a basic, but probably temporary, change in the economy of the United States. The best term for the new economy is "defense economy." The essential characteristics of the defense economy are three: (1) the demand for goods is substantially too large for the productive capacity of the economy; (2) the large demand for goods is mainly the result of buying by the government; and (3) a variety of special controls are necessary in order to assure that defense goods are promptly produced and in order to prevent the huge demands for goods from causing a rapid rise in prices.

There have been numerous periods in which the demand for goods has been too large for the productive capacity of industry and when, as a result, the price level has risen. The defense economy is distinguished, however, by the fact that the demand for goods is *substantially* too large for supply. Consequently, special methods, such as priorities and allocations, are necessary to assure that defense goods are produced without delay and special controls are needed in order to keep the rise in prices moderate. The fact that the additional demand is caused largely by government buying and that government expenditures are abnormally high means that the government is confronted with difficult problems of financing its expenditures.

Although we must assume that the defense economy will be temporary, it may have lasting effects upon economic policies and institutions. People the country over are asking themselves whether the various controls developed during the defense economy — such as priorities and allocations, ceilings on prices, restraints on collective bargaining, taxes on excess profits — will become a permanent part of the American economy. Will the intervention of the government in economic affairs be made permanently greater than it otherwise would have been? Will the area of individual discretion be permanently narrowed?

In order to judge the lasting consequences, we must try to arrive at estimates of the size of military expenditures and the duration and principal characteristics of the defense economy.

THE SIZE OF DEFENSE EXPENDITURES

In his speech on September 9, 1950, President Truman announced that by June 1951 the country would be spending at the annual rate of 30 billion dollars a year on defense. Then came the acceleration of rearmament. During the calendar year 1951, domestic military outlays and foreign military aid (in terms of late 1950 dollars) will probably be in the neighborhood of 40 billion dollars, or a little more than one seventh of the net national product. No official estimate has been published concerning the size of defense expenditures in 1952 and 1953, but they will probably be slightly above 50 billion dollars a year in terms of late 1950 dollars.[1] This would be about one sixth of the net national product. Outlays on defense are subject to large and sudden

[1] Throughout this chapter figures referring to the national product, expenditures on defense, and goods available for consumption will be in terms of dollars of the purchasing power of the third quarter of 1950.

changes as a result of developments in international relations, but it is important to remember that the demand for defense goods is at all times held back by the rapid improvement of military equipment and by the reluctance of the armed services to spend large amounts for equipment that will soon be obsolete.

If relations between the United States and Russia continue bad, this country will maintain a large number of men under arms for an indefinite period. The number will depend upon the areas that this country elects to defend, our success in persuading other countries to defend themselves, and developments in the art of warfare. The United States, however, will have considerable difficulty in maintaining, over extended periods, a military force of more than 3 million or 4 million men. About one million males reach the age of eighteen each year, and of this number about 800,000 would be fit for military service if standards were slightly reduced. A two-year term of service would produce an armed force of about 1.6 million. A longer term than twenty-four months would probably be impracticable in an armed peace. The additional men needed for a military force of 3 million or 4 million would have to be obtained by hiring professionals. The government would not find it easy to hire as many as 2 million professionals for the armed services.

Even if the number of men in the armed services remains indefinitely at about 3 million, the outlay on defense is likely to drop after two to four years to between 30 billion and 40 billion dollars a year in terms of late 1950 dollars. This would be roughly one tenth of the net national product.

The reason for the ultimate drop in expenditures is that exceptionally large outlays will be necessary for the next two or three years while the armed services are being supplied with original equipment. After several years, however, outlays for equipment will be governed in the main by the need for replacements and improvements. The estimate of 30 billion to 40 billion dollars a year is based on recent experience, which shows defense outlays of a little less than 10,000 dollars per year (in terms of 1950 dollars) per man in the armed services and on the assumptions that outlays per man will rise as more and more equipment is used but that foreign military aid will drop substantially.[2]

The Duration of the Defense Economy

How long is the defense economy likely to last? In answering this question, one needs to consider both the ab-

[2] Recent defense expenditures in relation to the size of the armed forces were as follows:

	Defense expenditures in current dollars (billions)	Armed forces (thous.)	Expenditures per man-year in current dollars	Expenditures per man-year in 1950 dollars
1946	$21.1	3,300	$6,394	$8,701
1947	12.7	1,440	8,819	9,544
1948	11.2	1,307	8,569	8,493
1949	12.9	1,466	8,799	9,195

In 1941, 1942, 1943, and 1944, when much original equipment was being supplied the armed services, expenditures per man-year were much larger. In terms of 1950 dollars they were $16,044 in 1941, $21,100 in 1942, $14,467 in 1943, and $11,652 in 1944.

normal underlying economic conditions that make the defense economy different from a normal economy and the policies and controls that accompany the defense economy. The disappearance of the extraordinary economic conditions that require special controls will not necessarily mean that the controls will be promptly terminated.

More or less normal underlying economic conditions will return when there is no longer a substantial shortage of nearly all kinds of goods. This change is likely to occur soon after the outlay on armaments shifts pretty largely to a replacement basis. At that time defense expenditures should drop by about 10 to 20 billion dollars a year. About two or three years will probably be required to provide the enlarged armed services with adequate and up-to-date equipment. The precise period will depend upon the amount of the increase in our military forces, the consumption and destruction of equipment in local military operations, and the changes in the art of warfare.

It may be that the substantial shortages that are characteristic of the defense economy will not promptly disappear as soon as expenditures on armaments shift to a replacement basis. During the period of high defense expenditures, unsatisfied demand for many goods may accumulate, just as it did during the Second World War. Deferred demand will be particularly large if price controls cause a drop in quality and produce shortages of the kinds of goods that consumers most desire. The postponed demand may be merely large enough to facilitate the transition from a defense economy to a more or less normal peacetime economy; or it may be so large and so urgent as to continue the danger of inflation even after spending on defense drops to a more or less "normal" level.

How Much Can Production Be Increased?

The possibility of increasing production during the defense economy depends upon four basic conditions: (1) increase in the labor force; (2) reduction in the amount of unemployment; (3) increase in the length of the work week; and (4) rise in output per man-hour. During the Second World War the rapid rise in output astonished everyone. Indeed, production increased so enormously that the quantity of consumer goods available for civilian use was actually greater during the war than it had been before the war—in 1943 it was 12.5 per cent higher than in 1940, and in 1945 it was 28.4 per cent larger. No such great increase of goods for consumption can be expected during the defense economy. The gain after 1940 was made possible by several conditions. There was an expansion of the labor force by 9 million, a reduction in unemployment of 7 million, and an increase of about one sixth in the length of the work week. The large rise in employment, in turn, was made possible by the abundance of the supplies of most raw materials and by the fact that in many industries there was, in 1940, considerable unused capacity. The increase in the output of consumer goods was partly made possible by keeping the physical volume of construction and output of producers' durable equipment for private use at less than the low levels of 1939.

But no comparable possibilities for increasing the size of the labor force or reducing unemployment now exist, although some increase in the labor force and some reduction in unemployment is possible. Furthermore, it is important, in contrast to the 1941–1945 period, to maintain a high rate of expenditures on plant and equipment, thus raising the productive capacity of the economy.

On the basis of moderately optimistic assumptions concerning the determinants of output, one may conclude that the net national output will rise from about 260 billion dollars in 1950 to 284 billion in 1951 and 300 billion in 1952. The assumptions on which these figures rest are: that the labor force increases from about 64.6 million in 1950 to 66.1 million in 1951 and 67.1 million in 1952; that unemployment drops from 3.1 million in 1950 to 1.5 million in 1951 and 1952; that there is a small increase of about 4 per cent in the average weekly working hours between 1950 and 1951 and another 2 per cent between 1951 and 1952; that there is no change in output per man-hour between 1950 and 1951; and that there is a normal increase of 2.5 per cent in output per man-hour between 1951 and 1952. Output per worker per year (in terms of third quarter of 1950 dollars) would rise on the basis of these assumptions from a little more than 4200 dollars in 1950 to slightly more than 4400 dollars in 1951 and 4600 dollars in 1952.

A rise in the net national product from 260 billion dollars in 1950 to 284 billion in 1951 and 300 billion in 1952, and an increase in defense expenditures and foreign military aid to about 40 billion dollars in 1951 and 50 billion in 1952 would mean a slight drop in the quantity of goods available for nondefense purposes between 1950 and 1951 and a moderate rise between 1951 and 1952. There would, however, be a drop of about 5 billion dollars, as an annual rate, between the third quarter of 1950 and the year 1951 in the quantity of goods available for nondefense purposes.

Somewhat less optimistic assumptions concerning the possible increase in the labor force or in the length of the work week indicate a net national product of about 276 billion dollars in 1951. These less optimistic assumptions are that the labor force increases by only one million between 1950 and 1951, and the length of the work week by only 2 per cent. This smaller rise in the net national product, if accompanied by an increase in defense expenditures from 14 billion to 40 billion dollars, would leave about 10 billion dollars less goods available for nondefense purposes than in 1950.

Let us look briefly at the production potentials of the defense economy.

1. *The possibility of increasing the size of the labor force.* The labor force in the defense economy will be a higher proportion of people of working age than in the normal peacetime economy. Until about 1940, there had been a tendency for the ratio of males of working age in the labor force to decline — this tendency being due partly to a rise in the age of entering industry and partly to earlier retirements. On the other hand, the ratio of women of working age in the labor force has long been rising. The drop in the proportion of males of working age in the labor force probably came to an end about 1940, and the ratio will gradually increase. This tendency will be accentuated by

the strong demand for labor in the defense economy. Retirements of older workers will be postponed and many retired men will return to the labor force. Particularly important will be the return to active responsibilities of many able executives, engineers, and other professional workers who have retired within the last four or five years. The strong demand for labor will undoubtedly accelerate the increase in the proportion of women of working age in industry.

The normal increase in the labor force from 1950 to 1951 would be about 600,000. This assumes that there is no change in the ratio between the labor force and the population of working age. If the proportion of males of 65 years of age or more in the labor force were to rise from about 45 per cent to 55 per cent, and if the proportion of women of 44 years of age or more in the labor force should continue to increase at the same rate as between 1949 and 1950, the labor force would increase by about 1.1 million between 1950 and 1951. Men in the armed services are counted as in the labor force. The draft and enlistments, therefore, will bring into the labor force some persons who would not otherwise be counted in it because they were in school rather than employed. This addition to the labor force may be as high as 400,000, making the rise in the labor force between 1950 and 1951 about 1.5 million. In the year 1952 the increase in the labor force would be less, probably not more than about 1 million.

2. *The possibility of reducing unemployment.* In the war year of 1944, unemployment averaged only 670,000, and in 1943 and 1945 it was about 1 million. In the postwar

boom years of 1947 and 1948 it was about 2.1 million and
in the busy third quarter of 1950, 2.7 million. Labor shortages in the defense economy will be very acute. Hence it
is reasonable to assume that unemployment will be some-
where between the war years of 1943 or 1945 and the
postwar boom years of 1947 or 1948 — say, about 1.5 million.

3. *The possibility of increasing hours per week.* Stiff pen-
alties on the employer for work beyond 40 hours per week
naturally tend to limit the length of the work week. In
the boom years of 1947 and 1948 the average work
week in manufacturing was 40.4 hours and 40.1
hours. And yet under the pressure of war it had risen to
44.9 hours in 1943 and 45.2 hours in 1944. In 1950 the work
week in manufacturing averaged a little more than 40
hours. A moderately optimistic assumption is that the work
week for the labor force as a whole in 1951 will average
about 4 per cent above 1950 and that in 1952 it will be
about 2 per cent longer than in 1951. On the other hand, the
increase in the length of the work week will be retarded
by widespread shortages of raw materials. One reason why
a big jump occurred in the work week in the durable goods
industries during the Second World War was that most
raw materials were in good supply. The steel industry, for
example, was able to increase the output of ingots by nearly
one third between 1940 and 1943. No comparable increase
is in prospect today.

4. *The possibility of an increase in output per man-hour.*
Output per man-hour, which normally increases about 2.5
per cent per year, is not likely to be any higher in 1951

than in 1950 — partly because many experienced workers will be lost to the armed services, partly because many new and inexperienced persons will be entering employment, partly because there will be an abnormally large number of shifts from one kind of work to another, partly because the production of many kinds of war goods will be in the tooling-up stage or will not yet be running smoothly, and partly because production will be held back by shortages of material and technical personnel. For example, the Engineering Manpower Commission of the Engineers' Joint Council reported that by December 1950 the average company among a group of large and important concerns (virtually all of them engaged in vital defense production) had lost 10 per cent of its engineering personnel by either the draft or the activation of reservists. The difficulties of increasing output per man-hour or per worker are indicated by the experience of 1950. Although weekly working hours were greater in the third quarter than in the first, output per nongovernment worker in the third quarter, expressed in dollars of constant purchasing power, was the same as in the first quarter — it was running at the rate of $4491 per year as compared with $4475 in the first quarter. These figures cannot be regarded as accurate, but the fact that they indicate no change in output per worker during 1950 is significant. Between 1951 and 1952 output per man-hour may rise by the normal amount because many inexperienced workers will by then have been trained and many obstacles to defense production will have been overcome.

SOME CHARACTERISTICS OF THE DEFENSE ECONOMY

The training of semiskilled workers, and to a less extent skilled, will be encouraged, but the training of scientists, engineers, doctors, and other professional men will be hindered. The great expansion of production in the heavy industries, the large losses of workers to the armed services, and the entrance of a large number of inexperienced persons into the labor force will stimulate the training of semiskilled workers. The need may not be as large as it was during the Second World War but it will, nevertheless, be substantial. The training of skilled workers, on balance, will probably also be encouraged — though much less so than the training of the semiskilled. A strong demand for labor always encourages the training of skilled workers. The need for additional skilled operators in a hurry will often cause the training of semiskilled specialists to be preferred to the training of skilled workers. Nevertheless, this need will also cause training methods to be improved and the length of the training courses to be reduced. The armed services themselves require large numbers of skilled workers and will be a source of training.

Unfortunately, the draft will reduce the annual output of scientists, engineers, doctors, and other professional workers. This is most regrettable because the security of the country requires that the number of these workers be substantially increased. There is no reason, except political timidity, why arrangements should not be worked out to increase the number trained during the defense period. But political timidity is a powerful influence and, in spite of the urgent need for more scientists and professional workers, the number trained will drop. The Engineering Manpower Commission of the Engineers' Joint Council has estimated that the number of new engineers needed each year is around 30,000. Estimates of enrollment trends in engineering schools made before the outbreak of war in Korea indicated that the graduates of engineering schools would soon fall below 20,000 a year. By 1954, the Engineering Manpower Commission estimates that there will be a cumulative shortage of over 40,000 engineering graduates. This does not take account of the effect of the accelerated draft that began late in 1950. Already industry is suffering from a serious shortage of engineers of five to ten years' experience, due to the virtual cessation of engineering training during the Second World War. The Engineering Manpower Commission points out that Russia during the last five years has trained more engineers than the United States.

To some extent the drop in the number of scientists, engineers, and other professional workers can be offset by an increase in the number of women entering these fields. Such an increase will undoubtedly occur. Since women have not been in the habit of going into these fields, the increase in the number of women scientists, engineers, physicians, and architects will probably be slow. Furthermore, the defense economy will probably have been replaced by a more or less normal economy before many women will have been graduated from courses in science, engineering, or medicine.

Research in basic science will probably be retarded.

Some of the research on technological problems will undoubtedly indirectly help the advance of pure science. Nevertheless, the shift of many men who might be working on pure science to technological research will undoubtedly retard the development of pure science.

Technological research will probably be encouraged. There is no doubt that the demand for technological research in the defense economy will be far greater than in a normal peacetime economy. The greatest growth in demand will come from the various armed services, but there will also be a great rise in the demand for research by business enterprises. This latter demand will be stimulated by material shortages, by pressure of rising labor costs against price ceilings, by production problems arising in the making of defense goods, and by the excess profits tax. The output of technological research will be increased by five principal methods: (1) shifting men from work on pure science to work on technological problems; (2) shifting men from teaching to research; (3) recalling retired research workers to active duty; (4) increasing the tempo of research and the number of hours put on research by research workers; (5) providing research workers more liberally with apparatus and assistance. Technological research will, of course, be discouraged to some extent by the loss of students in science and engineering to the armed services.

The defense economy will be a period of rising prices. Personal incomes after taxes are bound to rise considerably faster during the next two years than the physical output of consumer goods. Part of the growth of personal incomes will go into savings. One important kind of personal saving will be the repayment of debts. At the end of 1950, non-corporate debts were about 100 billion dollars in comparison with 55.4 billion at the end of 1945.[3] Part of the growth in incomes after taxes will go into higher prices for consumer goods. Just how rapidly prices advance will depend upon the nature and effectiveness of price controls. There are two schools of thought about the control of prices. Some people believe that main reliance should be placed on so-called "indirect" controls — reduction in government spending, higher taxes, strict control of credit, and the encouragement of saving. Others would rely upon direct controls — that is, ceilings on prices and wages.

The efficacy of both indirect and direct controls is limited. Indirect controls have two important limitations. One shortcoming is that they affect only the demand for goods. The price level, however, depends partly upon costs and sooner or later must adjust itself to changes in costs. In a strong sellers' market, unions are able to push up wages rapidly, and they have been doing so ever since the outbreak of the fighting in Korea. Some indirect controls are actually likely to encourage the demands for wage increases. This is true of general sales taxes and even of broad increases in income taxes. It does not follow that a general sales tax is undesirable in times of threatened inflation; it is a tax on spending and thus tends to increase the proportion of incomes saved. But a general sales tax tends to raise prices, particularly in a sellers' market.

[3] In relation to personal incomes after taxes, individual and non-corporate debts, however, were actually smaller in 1950 than ten years earlier.

Some indirect methods of control, such as taxes on corporate profits, fail to limit the rise in the prices of consumer goods because they have little effect upon the tendency for personal incomes after taxes to outrun the supply of consumer goods. The idea behind increases in corporate taxes is that they would cause corporate expenditures on plant and equipment to be reduced, thus releasing productive capacity for making consumer goods. At a time when the United States is engaged in a production contest with Russia, forcing a reduction in expenditures on plant and equipment would be a blunder.

As a matter of fact, however, higher corporate taxes will probably have little effect on expenditures on plant and equipment. These expenditures will be determined by the availability of labor and supplies. Increases in corporate income taxes will encourage corporations to raise prices or to reduce the quality of goods. If necessary, the funds to finance higher outlays on plant and equipment will be obtained by borrowing from banks or by selling part of the large holdings of government securities now owned by corporations — each an inflationary method.

The efficacy of direct controls is also limited. Price ceilings may limit inflation, but they do not entirely prevent it — in large part they conceal it, or temporarily postpone it. Inflation takes the form of reduction in quality, of the shift of transactions to the black market, of the failure of industry to make the kind and quality of goods that the market demands. But to the extent that consumers cannot buy the kind and quality of goods that they desire, they increase their saving. Thus the demand for goods is temporarily limited.

Ceilings on wages also are of limited effectiveness. They tend to produce evasions in the form of fictitious up-grading of workers, of increases for this and that group to remove suddenly discovered "inequities," of all manner of demands for compensation in other forms — more paid holidays, travel time, higher rates for call-in time, higher pensions or sick benefits, rules that compel the employer to pay higher penalty overtime rates.

It must not be inferred from the limitations on both indirect and direct controls that a reasonably effective check to inflation is impossible. A combination of strict indirect controls and of restraints on wage increases would probably suffice to hold the real rise in prices to 5 per cent a year or less. Restraints on wage increases might take the form of restrictions of wage advances to (1) quarterly adjustments to meet changes in the cost of living and (2) such other advances as may be essential to promote the output of defense goods. Since there is no complete assurance that the rise in prices can be prevented, wage earners are entitled to adjustments in their wages that do not exceed changes in the cost of living. But at a time when consumer incomes are outrunning the supply of consumer goods, workers are not entitled to wage increases that exceed the rise in living costs. Strict indirect controls would mean substantial reductions in unessential government spending, increases in personal income taxes, strict control of consumer credit and real estate credit, and vigorous efforts to encourage saving. A well-conceived plan to encourage saving would involve offering would-be savers a variety of government securities carefully designed to meet the needs of different kinds of savers.

If the rise in prices were held to 5 per cent a year or less, controls would be more effective than during the Second World War. Between 1940 and 1942 the consumers' price index advanced 17.2 per cent. During the next three years, 1942–1945, the rise was somewhat slower — only 13.4 per cent.[4] The actual increase in living costs was somewhat greater than the index showed because a large part of the meat was sold in black markets. Furthermore, there was a good deal of suppressed inflation because rising labor costs were not fully reflected in the consumers' price index between 1942 and 1945, but did affect prices when controls were removed after the war. Furthermore, between 1942 and 1945, controls were least effective in the areas where they

---

[4] These figures differ somewhat from the changes in the official consumers' price index because they represent a rough adjustment of the index to take account of the understatement of price increases during the price-control period. The adjustment was made by the technicians of the Council of Economic Advisers and is based upon the report of the Technical Committee (known as the Mitchell Committee) on the consumers' price index. The adjusted figures are published in the *Midyear Economic Report of the President,* July 1950, p. 122. The adjusted figures do not take into account black market prices, that is, the prices charged by persons who intentionally evaded ceilings, but they do attempt to take into account the so-called "gray market" prices, that is, violations of ceilings caused by ignorance. There were a great many such violations, although the differences between the gray market prices and ceiling prices were usually not very large.

were most needed, namely in the case of prices of food and apparel.

Although the control of prices ought to be more effective than during the Second World War, lack of determination and political courage will probably make the control less effective. At whatever point the government attacks the problem of inflation, it meets strong resistance. The trade unions object to direct restraints on wages unless prices are effectively controlled. Direct controls of prices, as I have indicated, are not effective except in limited areas. The use of so-called indirect methods of control also meets strong resistance. Consequently, the application of indirect controls has been timid and, in part, misdirected. Stiffer increases in taxes have been imposed on corporations than on individuals — though only increases in the personal income tax limit the demand for consumers' goods. The government has lacked a program for encouraging saving and has been unwilling to offer individuals securities that they would buy eagerly in place of consumers' goods. During the period from July 1 to November 1, 1950, when consumer expenditures were rising rapidly, and when the government should have been encouraging saving, redemptions of E bonds exceeded purchases by nearly 400 million dollars.

The indirect controls will probably be gradually improved and somewhat stiffened, but there is little prospect that they will prevent consumer expenditures from rising faster than the physical output of consumer goods. In particular, the prices of most foodstuffs are likely to rise. Ceilings on such prices are ineffective. Furthermore, the law prohibits the imposition of ceilings on any food or agricultural product until prices exceed so-called "parity" or the highest price charged between May 24 and June 24, 1950. "Parity" means the ratio between the prices received by farmers and the prices paid by farmers during either 1910–1914 or the most recent ten years, whichever is higher. The prices of many farm products are still below parity and the formula makes parity rise as the prices of nonagricultural products increase.

The defense economy will be to some extent a period of suppressed inflation. The expression "suppressed inflation" as I am using it here means that prices have been held down to a lower level than demand and costs will in the long run justify. Ceilings on prices are quite likely (though not certain) to produce suppressed inflation. The danger of suppressed inflation is less when wages as well as prices are held down. If costs have not risen, supply can eventually adjust itself to ceiling prices. On the other hand, if wages are held down less strictly than prices, as was done during the Second World War, when straight-time wage rates in manufacturing rose about 35 per cent between 1941 and 1945, and the price level of consumer goods about 27 per cent, a subsequent adjustment of the price level to the wage level or of the wage level to the price level is inevitable. During the defense economy the rise in hourly earnings will be greater than the rise in the consumers' price index — though not necessarily less than the rise in the real cost of living. After the transition to a somewhat normal economy, the price level will adjust itself to the rise in the wage level.

The standard of consumption in the country as a whole will drop very little during the defense economy, and the drop will not be of long duration. I have estimated that the net national product in 1951 might be from 275 to 284 billion dollars, in terms of dollars of third quarter of 1950 purchasing power, and about 16 billion dollars a year more in 1952. If domestic military expenditures and foreign aid are about 40 billion dollars in 1951 and 50 billion in 1952, the output available for nonmilitary outlays will be from 235 to 244 billion dollars in 1951 and 241 to 251 billion dollars in 1952. In 1950, the output available for nonmilitary expenditures was about 244 billion dollars.

The quantity of goods available for consumption will depend upon the purchases of nonmilitary goods by the government and the volume of private investment. Purchases of nonmilitary goods by the local, state, and national governments are not likely to drop. There will, of course, be cuts or postponements of some kinds of expenditures because of shortages of materials. On the other hand, other types of expenditures, more or less indirectly related to military requirements, will increase. This is true of highways, air raid shelters, water supply, and possibly hospitals.

There will be a fairly substantial drop in the large outlays on housing. Cuts in the output of housing and of durable consumer goods, such as automobiles and various household articles, will probably permit the increase and improvement of plant and equipment to continue at close to the high rate of 1950. All of this indicates that the total volume of goods available for personal consumption will be little different in 1951 from 1950, though somewhat smaller than the volume available in the second half of 1950. It also indicates that the volume of goods available for consumption in 1952 may be a little bit higher than in 1951 — though this last assertion assumes only a limited rise in military expenditures in 1951 and 1952. When account is taken of the rise in population, the quantity of goods available for consumption per capita will compare less favorably with 1950.

Although the total quantity of goods available for consumption will probably be about as large in 1951 as in 1950, and somewhat larger in 1952 than in 1950, the quality will frequently be poorer and the *kinds* of goods will not conform to the preferences of consumers as did the output in 1950. The supplies of new automobiles, television sets, refrigerators, houses, and many other durable consumer goods will be substantially less than in 1950. The drop in quality and the limited range of choice will cause a large proportion of consumers to feel that their standard of living has dropped — and they will be right. The experience of the community in 1951 and 1952 will illustrate how important are the kinds of goods produced as well as the mere quantity of output.

The distribution of the standard of living in 1951 and 1952 will differ in important respects from 1950. Part of the population will enjoy a rise in its standard of living and part will suffer a fall. The persons who gain most will be the ones who otherwise would not have been employed — those who represent the drop in the unemployment rate and the increase in the labor force. The groups that will enjoy the next largest gains will be the politically favored ones such as the farmers; people in a strong bargaining position, such as trade union members; and many of the self-employed whose activities are not easily regulated by the government. The groups that will lose are the unorganized white-collar workers and the recipients of income in the form of interest and probably in the form of rent.

The volume of personal savings, and the ratio of personal savings to personal incomes after taxes, will rise. This will be one of the results of the tendency for personal incomes after taxes to outrun the physical volume of consumer goods. The more effectively black markets are prevented and the greater the shortages of the kind and quality of goods that consumers desire, the greater will be the increase in the volume of personal savings.

The growth in personal savings, combined with the prospect that the price level will rise, will create a difficult investment problem for many savers. I have indicated that some savers will be able to solve this problem by repaying debts. Others will be able to meet the problem by investing in houses or unincorporated businesses. The volume of new housing construction will drop substantially, but the capacity of housing to absorb savings will not drop in proportion. Much housing construction during the last two years has been financed by the expansion of bank credit. During the defense economy, housing will undoubtedly be financed to a greater extent out of personal savings. Issues of equity securities by corporations may rise slightly, but little help for the individual investor can be counted on from an increase in new corporate issues.

During the Second World War a substantial part of personal savings took the form of personal holdings of cash and demand deposits, which increased from 11.4 billion dollars at the end of 1939 to 45.7 billion dollars at the end of 1945. In December 1939, 42.7 per cent of all non-government holdings of cash and demand deposits belonged to individuals; in December 1945, this proportion had risen to 53.3 per cent. Individuals suffered heavy losses from the drop in the purchasing power of their cash and demand deposits. Of course, persons who invested in bonds or savings bank deposits also suffered a loss, but they received partial compensation from the interest on their bonds or savings bank deposits.

The unfortunate experiences of individuals during the Second World War may produce a change in their behavior during the defense period. They may be less willing to accumulate cash and demand deposits and may seek to obtain partial protection against the rise in prices by making investments that at least bear interest. The deficits in the Federal budget will produce an increase in the supply of bonds. The Federal government may take advantage of the plight of the individual saver by offering bonds that pay only an extremely low rate of interest. Indeed, there will be a sharp contrast in the government's treatment of wage earners, who are organized and aggressive and have political influence, and in its treatment of savers, who are not organized. The government will permit wages to be adjusted for increases in the cost of living but will not be easily persuaded to give equivalent treatment to savers by offering them bonds payable in a fixed amount of purchasing power.

Corporate profits will drop. This will be the result of price controls, of increases in wages and in the corporate income tax that are not completely passed on in the form of higher prices or lower quality, and of the excess-profits tax. One may ask whether the drop in corporate profits will prevent corporations from financing a high rate of expenditures on plant and equipment. I do not believe that this result will follow. As I have indicated above, expenditures on plant and equipment can be financed in part by sales of government bonds owned by corporations. Accelerated depreciation will help enterprises in defense industries pay for large outlays on plant and equipment. Some corporations will conserve cash by paying dividends in stock and some will resort to borrowing from bankers. The expansion of plant and equipment will be limited by labor and materials, not by funds.

The ratio of the Federal debt to the net national product will drop. In 1950, when the gross Federal debt was about 260 billion dollars, the net national product was also about 260 billion. Let us assume that the peak of defense production comes in the calendar year 1953. The budget of the Federal government will show a small deficit in the fiscal year 1950–1951, and a larger but still moderate deficit in the next two fiscal years. The deficit will be kept down by the high yield of taxes made possible by the high income levels of the several years ahead. The total increase in the Federal debt in the next three years will probably be less than 40 billion dollars. In the meantime the price level will probably have risen by 15 to 20 per cent above the average for 1950. Consequently, the net national product by

1953, in current dollars, should be well in excess of 350 billion dollars, making the ratio of debt to product considerably less than it is today.

The ratio of interest charges on the Federal debt to the net national product may not decline, and might possibly rise by a small amount. The Treasury seems quite willing to risk a rise in prices in order to keep interest rates low. It will probably have to recede somewhat from this position, but it will do so only with reluctance and under pressure. The safest conclusion is that the ratio of interest payments on the Federal debt to the net national product will show little change up or down.

THE LASTING EFFECTS OF THE DEFENSE ECONOMY

What will be the lasting effects of the defense economy? One of its most important results will be to strengthen and accelerate developments that would have occurred anyway. For example, organized industrial research will be more broadly established in industry than ever before, and its value will be better appreciated. As soon as personnel is available, the spread of research and engineering departments into concerns of medium size will be accelerated. The tendency to raise the usual age of retirement at least among nonexecutive positions will be re-enforced. So also will be the tendency for women to enter the physical sciences, medicine, and engineering. The plight of the thrifty during the defense economy will probably lead to some small broadening of the ownership of corporations — a development that would have sooner or later occurred anyway. Price controls, taxes, and advancing wages will make corporations more dependent on outside funds to finance expansion. The prospect of rising prices will make borrowing from banks, insurance companies, and pension funds attractive, but some concerns will take advantage of the opportunity to get more stockholders. Union membership will spread, especially among white-collar workers, who will discover in many enterprises that the best way to get their wages adjusted for increases in the cost of living is to organize.

What will happen to taxes and to the various controls of materials, credit, prices, and wages? When spending for military equipment shifts to a replacement basis, the budget of the Federal government will show a surplus and the pressure for tax reductions will be strong. First consideration will probably be given the personal income tax. The excess-profits tax will probably be repealed. The special reasons for enacting it will have passed. Furthermore, as time passes the tax will become increasingly unjust and hard to defend. In a peacetime economy the unfavorable effects of an excess-profits tax upon employment opportunities and wages in expanding industries will be apparent. Hence, it would not be surprising to see even the unions join in the demand for repeal of the excess-profits tax. Little or no reduction in the tax on ordinary corporate income is likely — indeed, it may be necessary to raise the ordinary tax on corporate income in order to repeal the excess-profits tax. A general tax on corporate income has a strong appeal to politicians, because it seems to fall on corporations. As a matter of fact, it is soon passed on, and for that reason is a good tax. It is a levy, unlike the present personal income tax, that falls broadly upon the entire community.

The various controls of materials will not continue after shortages have passed. It remains to be seen whether control of consumer credit will survive the defense period. It did not long survive the Second World War, but it is badly needed and should have been in effect in the early half of 1950. Nevertheless, the control of consumer credit is unpopular. The man with a small income who wishes to buy an automobile, refrigerator, or television set on credit believes that he is entitled to just as liberal terms as the seller is willing to give him. Consequently, the Federal Reserve System will probably again lose its authority over the terms of consumer credit.

Will price controls be kept? I assume that they will be looser than they were during the Second World War. This will be necessary to avoid the maldistribution of goods, the drop in quality, and the rise of black markets that accompanied price controls then. They will bear more heavily on big business than on farmers and will be tighter on many nonnecessaries, such as automobiles, than on foodstuffs. Indeed, price controls may not apply very generally to foodstuffs. Although price controls will probably be so administered as to make them less objectionable than they became during the Second World War, they will probably not long survive the drop in defense expenditures that will occur when the buying of military equipment shifts to a replacement basis. Either they will be administered more and more laxly so that the case for keeping them becomes less and less convincing or their tendency to prevent producers from supplying the kind and quality of goods that buyers prefer will make price controls increasingly objectionable.

A more or less serious controversy over the removal of price controls may be generated if restraints on wage advances under the defense economy are much milder than restraints on price increases. The knowledge that the removal of price controls will permit the price level to adjust itself to the wage level will strengthen the opposition to the removal of price controls. The problem will be aggravated by the postponed inflation caused by the increase in the work week during the peak of defense production. When the work week drops, employees will expect compensating wage advances — as in 1946. The problem of dropping price controls will be aggravated also, if wage controls are removed before price controls — as happened after the Second World War. But although the removal of price controls may produce a rise in prices accompanied by the efforts of unions to get compensating wage increases that in turn produce some rise in prices, I do not believe that a general system of price controls can be kept long after the government's expenditures on defense have substantially dropped.

Will the community be led by the strong bargaining position of the trade unions during the defense economy to create permanent machinery for making and enforcing a national wage policy and for controlling the operation of collective bargaining? Probably not. Sooner or later the country may have to face the fact that strong trade unions, well established in all important industries, are bound to push up wages so fast that the community must have a slowly rising price level. Perhaps a decade of rising prices will be necessary before the community discovers that it must choose between accepting a creeping inflation and regulating collective bargaining. The defense economy will be too abnormal to cause people to draw inferences from it concerning the normal effects of collective bargaining upon the price level.

Some people fear that the widespread intervention by the government in economic matters during the defense economy will cause the community to look more and more to the government to guide and control economic activities. There is a long-run tendency for government intervention in economic matters to increase. I do not believe that this tendency will be accelerated to an appreciable extent by the defense economy. Most of the government intervention that will be induced by the defense economy will not be the kind that will breed the demand for more intervention. Most of the controls that accompany the defense economy are more or less unpopular — they are instituted only under the pressure of real or imagined necessity. That is why they are undertaken timidly, on too small a scale, and too late.

There will be a few exceptions to the generalization that the interference with normal economic activities which the government undertakes in the interest of national security are unpopular. But these exceptions will not be many. One of them is supplied by the government's efforts to adjust industrial disputes in order to prevent interruption to defense production. The staff of mediators that the government builds will make it better prepared after the defense emergency has passed to assist employers and unions to settle their differences. The government's help in adjusting industrial disputes seems to be gaining in favor.

The defense economy may have important and more or less lasting effects upon the political influence of groups that are important in making economic policies, and it may alter in important ways the attitude of the public toward the government. Both the farmers and the trade unions are likely to lose political influence as a result of experiences during the defense economy. The political influence of the farmers is likely to suffer from their prosperity and their success in winning special treatment for themselves in the formulation of price control policies. Their influence will not drop in the predominantly agricultural states, and they will undoubtedly continue to receive substantial subsidies from the government. Nevertheless, their claims for help will fall on less sympathetic ears and representatives of city dwellers will be less inclined to see their constituents taxed in order to keep the prices of farm products high.

The rise in the membership of unions will probably not be accompanied by a gain in their political influence. In fact, unions may lose a little of their great influence. During the defense economy they will do many things that will impress the public with their great economic strength. They will succeed, for example, in raising the standard of living of their members while the living standards of the rest of the community are remaining unchanged or going down. Stoppages that threaten to halt essential defense production are likely to be a problem. For some time the public has been slowly changing its attitude toward unions. At one time it regarded unions as weak organizations that were entitled to special privileges and special protection. The community is gradually becoming aware of the enormous economic power possessed by the strongest unions and of the need for placing restraints on the use of this power. Events during the defense economy will cause more and more people to become aware of the great economic power of unions, and this will be bad for the political influence of unions.

Particularly interesting is the possibility that the defense economy may bring a far-reaching change in the attitude of people toward the government. For some time a large part of the community has been inclined to look upon the government as a source for help without inquiring too closely how or where the government gets its means for giving help. This disposition to regard the government as a sort of Santa Claus has been encouraged by many politicians. During the defense economy, however, the government will not find it easy to play the role of Santa Claus. It will be required to make extraordinary demands upon individuals for heavy tax payments. The government, of course, will continue to be an important source of help to the needy, and to groups with strong political power, and government aid of various kinds will be given on an increasing scale. Nevertheless, the stiff demand for taxes during the defense economy will bring home to many persons an awareness of the fact that the people support the government; not the government, the people. It will probably bring closer the day when claims for special help are scrutinized with some objectivity and are subjected to criteria of fairness.

CHAPTER III

Some Probable Characteristics of the Economy in the Foreseeable Future

SOME CHARACTERISTICS of the economy of the future and some trends seem much more probable than others. A few of the most important and most probable I have selected for brief discussion in this chapter. These are trends that, even before the Korean war, seemed likely to occur. The war has not changed this prospect, but in some cases it is accelerating the expected developments.

COMMITMENT OF THE COMMUNITY TO A HIGH-LEVEL EMPLOYMENT POLICY

To begin with, the community will continue to be committed to the policy of maintaining a high level of employment. Sooner or later the policy may be strongly questioned, modified or abandoned, but that does not seem to be an immediate likelihood. This policy, as I pointed out briefly in the first chapter, is really quite a radical change in thinking because it means putting high-level employment ahead of other objectives also of great importance. For example, it means tolerating a more or less constantly rising price level or imposing restraints on collective bargaining. An increasing price level, in turn, is equivalent to the expropriation of considerable amounts of property in the form of savings deposits, bonds, rights to annuities, and life insurance.

Actually, for some years the policy of full employment will probably require little specific implementation. Even after the enlarged armed services have been supplied with modern military equipment, and the need for many special controls has greatly diminished, the demand for goods will tax the productive capacity of the economy, and the strong bargaining position of unions will confront the country with rising prices — a very different set of problems from those that most people several years ago expected would confront the community after the Second World War.

RAPID TECHNOLOGICAL PROGRESS

One of the most certain trends will be growing reliance upon technological research. For some years expenditures on industrial research have been increasing rapidly. They were eight times as large in 1940 as in 1920, and they are now over twice as large as in 1940.

I pointed out in Chapter II that the defense economy will greatly encourage the growth of technological research and will cause the spread of research and engineering departments into concerns of medium size. But even if there had been no outbreak of war in Korea, such expansion would have been rapid. The Second World War produced an enormous amount of research by the government, so that even before the Korean war the government was spending far more for this purpose than was industry. The strength of trade unions and the upward pressure on wages further stimulate research. The spread of research is almost automatic, because discoveries by one enterprise bring further research by its rivals.

All of this means that the community will be good at developing new products and new industries. Recent years have brought into existence the rayon, the air-transport, the air-conditioning, the television, and the frozen-foods industries. It is impossible to foresee what new ones will arise, but there is not the least reason to expect that the finding of new products and new processes will cease or even slow down. Indeed, as in the war, the research done for the armed services will help indirectly to develop new products for civilian use and help to increase the number of industries in the country. Progress in the knowledge of metals is likely to be particularly rapid and important.

Most of the gains of technological progress will go to employees and the self-employed, in the form of higher wages and sustained prices, rather than to the community as a whole in the form of lower prices. This is not a new condition. During the last century or more, wages have moved upward most of the time fast enough to prevent technological advances from producing a drop in the general price level. Certainly with employees now organized into strong unions, there is no reason to expect such a drop. This assures that bondholders and other interest receivers, as such, will have little or no share in technological progress. Business owners *as a whole* (except the self-employed) are likely to fare only a little better than the interest receivers. In the quickly expanding industries, owners of the successful concerns will make large gains. The great majority of concerns in new industries, however, fail to survive, as the history of the automobile or of the radio reminds us. A fresh demonstration of this truth will soon be given by the television industry. The owners of the concerns that go under suffer heavy losses. Business owners as a whole (except as they derive labor income from operating their own concerns) share in the gains of technology's improvements only when the level of commodity prices rises faster than labor costs. Of course, *all* members of the community benefit as consumers from such advances since new kinds of goods become available or the quality of existing goods is improved. The fact that successful pioneers in developing new products and processes soon share a considerable part of their gains with imitators means that investments worth making from the standpoint of the community may not be profitable to the pioneering inventors. Hence the rest of the community is probably better off when investors in risky projects are unduly optimistic in their expectations of return.

GOVERNMENT SPENDING

The expenditures of the state, local, and national governments will be a high fraction of the national product. Indeed, the country will be fortunate if it can prevent these from growing faster than the national output. During several years after the enlarged armed services have been equipped and when defense expenditures are dropping, the high yield of the special defense taxes may produce a budget surplus. This surplus, however, is not likely to last long, partly because taxes will be cut and partly because expenditures by the Federal government will grow.

Large increases in expenditures will need to be made by the local and state governments. For example, great amounts must be spent for schools, to take care of the large increase in children of school age during the last decade. Likewise huge outlays should be made on roads to take care of the roughly one-third greater number of passenger cars and the double number of trucks since 1940.[1] The rapid increase in the consumption of water requires large new expenditures on water supply, and the growing impatience of the community with the pollution of streams requires large outlays on sewage disposal. Flood control, irrigation, and power development all call for considerably more government costs. Outlays on old-age pensions under the old-age and survivors' insurance plan will greatly increase as more persons become eligible for pensions, as coverage is extended to those classes of self-employed who are still excluded, and as pensions for skilled workers and

[1] It is unnecessary that all of these large expenditures on roads be made out of taxes. Adoption of the method of financing important through highways by tolls, as done by Pennsylvania and New Jersey, would simultaneously give substantial relief to taxpayers and open up one of the largest investment opportunities in the history of the country.

supervisory workers are made more adequate. By 1960 the number of persons receiving pensions under the Federal scheme will have doubled.

Finally, some form of sickness and disability insurance seems inevitable because the frequency and severity of disability is unpredictable in individual cases. The disability and sick-benefit plans negotiated by unions reach only a small fraction of employees and do not cover the self-employed. Hence a government plan is needed. It may not necessarily apply to minor ills, which people can finance out of ordinary income or savings, but it is needed for serious and catastrophic disabilities that may require costly treatment and that may incapacitate the victim for several years or possibly indefinitely. Sickness and disability insurance would add several billions a year to the expenditures of the government. This does not mean that the increased outlays on medical care would be a net burden on the community. Despite abuses in the practice of medicine, too little is probably spent today on keeping people in good health.

The present outlay of the government on pensions under the old-age and survivors' insurance plan is different from other government expenditures in that it is financed, not out of general revenues, but by a payroll tax levied for this specific purpose. The workers, who pay half of the payroll tax, become entitled to benefits as a matter of right and regardless of need. Sickness and disability insurance will presumably be financed in the same way. The receipts and expenditures of the pension scheme are not included in the administrative budget of the government. Nevertheless, I have counted them as government expenditures in asserting that the outlays of the government will rise. Even though not included in the administrative budget, the disbursements on pensions are determined by the law. Furthermore, the size of pension payments affects the amount of revenue that the government must raise by taxation.

Accompanying the large spending of the government there will probably be frequent deficits in the government budget. The years in which the budget is in the red will probably exceed the years in which it shows a surplus. The explanation is simple. Politicians can gain votes by making expenditures, but increases in taxes do not ordinarily win votes. Hence the politicians will always be more ready to spend than to tax. It is true that after the peak of rearmament expenditures has been passed, the Federal budget may show a surplus for a year or more. The reason is that some of the substantial tax increases brought about by the Korean war will probably be kept after defense expenditures subside. These tax rates (or even tax rates moderately below them) have a very high yield and will produce substantial increases in revenues as the national product rises — probably an increase in excess of three billion dollars a year. But two or three years of budget surpluses would undoubtedly produce cuts in taxes and increases in expenditures.

Even if the budget is more or less chronically in the red, the *burden* of debt will not necessarily increase. The burden of the debt is measured by the ratio between interest payments on the debt and the net national product. In 1950 the net national product and the debt of the Federal government, as I have pointed out in Chapter II, were each about 260 billion dollars. Hence, if the national product rises faster than the debt, the debt burden will decrease — unless there is a sufficient rise in the rate of interest paid on the debt. By the year 1960, the net national product ought to be about 372 billion in terms of 1950 dollars. (This assumes that output per man-hour will grow about as quickly as during the last fifty years.) In the absence of a major war, however, the Federal debt is not likely also to rise by 112 billion dollars during the next ten years. If it rises by 50 billion dollars and the net national product by 112 billion, the ratio of the debt to the national product will be reduced. The average rate of interest on the debt will rise, particularly as people become aware of the upward trend in the price level. As I pointed out in Chapter II, in discussing the short-run outlook for the debt burden, the advance in interest rates is not likely to be sufficient to raise significantly the ratio of interest payments to the net national product.

TRADE UNION MEMBERSHIP

Union membership will grow. The increase will be temporarily stimulated by the defense economy. It will continue, however, after defense expenditures have dropped. The rise in union membership will not be rapid. It is true that the present membership of about 14 million is less than half of the nonsupervisory and nontechnical employees of industry. Nevertheless, most of the workers who are easiest to organize now belong to unions. The increase in membership will be among workers in retailing, among white-collar workers, and among the workers in the South. The experience of Britain, Sweden, and other countries where unions are well established suggests that the ratio of union members to all nonsupervisory and nontechnical employees may never rise above that of 1 out of 2, or 2 out of 3. A ratio of 1 out of 2 at present would mean a total union membership of nearly 24 million; 2 out of 3, over 31 million. As unions become so powerful that the wages of nonunion members are promptly adjusted to changes in union wage scales, non-members see less and less reason for joining.

A MORE STABLE ECONOMY

Our economy will be more stable than it has been in the past. Progress in improving its stability has been great during the last twenty years — greater than is generally realized. Most of these gains will be retained, and they may be added to. This does not mean that prices will not rise, but it does mean that the rise in prices, if it occurs, will be relatively steady.

Many changes have contributed to the gains in stability. Some relate to business practices. Managements have learned how to operate with smaller inventories in relation to sales. Small inventories make for stability because they limit the period during which enterprises might meet current demand out of inventories. Businessmen today are more sophisticated than thirty years ago and less inclined to behave in ways that aggravate the ups and downs in business. For example, the continuation of a period of expansion is less likely to make managers expect a further continuation of expansion — in other words, it is less likely to make them more and more optimistic. (Unfortunately, it cannot be said that a continuation of a period of contraction makes them less and less likely to expect contraction to continue.) To the extent that businessmen avoid the errors of optimism and pessimism, the ups and downs of business will be mitigated.

Unemployment compensation, which now extends to about three jobs out of five, adds to stability because it prevents unemployment from causing a complete loss of income. Pension plans have the same effect — a considerable drop in the demand for labor would cause many men who have reached the age of retirement but who are still at work to be retired, on pensions. Important improvements have been made in the banking system, and banking difficulties in the future are not likely to aggravate the contraction of business as they have done in every severe depression of the past. Bank deposits are insured up to 10,000 dollars, the huge holdings of government securities by the banks provide a secondary reserve of unprecedented size, and the Federal Reserve Banks are now authorized to lend to member banks on any assets regarded as suitable by the member banks. The scarcity of paper eligible for rediscount that forced banks to dump good bonds in 1931 and 1932 and to refuse to renew loans cannot occur again. A revolutionary change, as I have pointed out, has occurred in the monetary system. No longer are short-term business debts the principal source of money supply, and no longer will the repayment of these debts reduce the money supply at the very times when this would do the most harm. Finally, government fiscal policy may be counted upon to be a stabilizing influence in periods of contraction.

Offsetting to some extent the progress that has been achieved in making the economy more stable are important new causes of instability. One of these is the growing use of consumer credit. In a period of business contraction the maturities of a large volume of short-term loans to consumers would greatly exceed the new loans made. The result would be to aggravate the drop in the demand for consumer goods, and thus to intensify the recession. There is a possibility too, as I have pointed out, that the government budget will run a deficit in periods of high employment — as it did in the fiscal year 1949-1950. A deficit at high employment is likely to be quite inflationary. Instability may be caused also by the great bargaining power of unions in such periods. If wage increases create the expectation of further price rises, the Federal Reserve authorities may have difficulty in preventing a large increase in short-term borrowing to finance the buying of goods in anticipation of a rise in prices. Such an expansion of speculative buying and short-term borrowing in advance of current needs would lay the foundation for a substantial drop in private demand.

Although the importance of the new causes for instability should not be underestimated, the changes that make the economy more stable seem to be more important than the changes that make it less stable. And there is a possibility that new controls will be applied to some of the new sources of instability. For example, sooner or later the controls on consumer credit, authorized as emergency measures during the Second World War and again in 1950, will probably be made permanent.

THE OUTLOOK FOR PRICES DURING THE NEXT DECADE

The movement of the price level after the period of re-armament will be upward — at least during *most* years in the next decade or so. The trade unions are likely to be strong enough to raise money wages faster than the increase in output per man-hour. This, of course, will require some rise in prices. There is a possibility that the success of unions in raising wages will be so great as to induce a public demand for experiment with some form of more or less permanent wage controls. An active conflict between the United States and Russia, with regional fighting from time to time, would put the unions in such a strong bargaining position that free collective bargaining would be intolerable. But if the conflict between the United States and Russia is not particularly active, the community, after its short ex-perience with direct controls during the period of rearma-ment, may tolerate rising labor costs for some years before it again experiments with direct controls.

The tendency for prices to rise will be re-enforced by the large expenditures of the government and the frequent deficits in the budget. Eventually the community may revolt against rising prices and make ambitious efforts to retard or prevent the increase. This possibility will be discussed in the next chapter. An effective revolt will probably not occur until the country has had some more years of experience with advancing prices.

The prospect that the movement of prices will be upward during most of the years immediately ahead raises difficult questions for many people and may require important changes in economic practices and institutions. For example, the prospect suggests that savings bank deposits, postal savings deposits, and the present type of government savings bond are no longer suitable long-term investments for most small savers. A solution of the investment problem of small savers in an economy with rising prices is not easily found. In some cases the problem may be solved, in part at least, by an investment in a farm or a house which is likely to rise in value as prices advance. To a considerable extent the shares of conservatively run investment trusts may take the place of savings bank deposits or government savings bonds. Possibly the government will issue savings bonds payable in a fixed amount of purchasing power.

A RISE IN THE PROPORTION OF THE POPULATION IN THE LABOR FORCE

I have pointed out in Chapter II that the needs of the defense economy will bring about an increase in the size of the labor force for the next several years. The long-run tendency, however, will also be for the labor force to become an increasing proportion of the population of working age. Between 1890 and 1940, the proportion of population of 14 years of age or more in the labor force showed little change —it was 53.4 per cent in 1890 and 54.1 per cent in 1940. There was a tendency for the proportion of males in the working force to drop, but this was offset by the rise in the proportion of women in the labor force. The strong demand for labor during the war and the postwar boom caused the labor force to rise by 1950 to 57.4 per cent of the population of 14 years of age or over.[2]

The labor force will continue to become an increasing proportion of the population of working age. Experience has shown that a strong demand for labor tends to swell the size of the labor force, and rapid technological change, tension between the United States and Russia, and the policy of encouraging a high level of employment will all tend to keep the demand for labor strong. In addition, the size of the labor force will be increased by the growing popularity of working, especially among married women and older workers. This popularity of working has been increased by a variety of conditions: improvements in working condi-

[2] The proportion of population of working age in the labor force at several dates was as follows:

	Population of 14 years of age and over (millions)	Labor force (millions)	Percentage of population of working age in the labor force
June 1890	41.8	22.3	53.4
June 1900	51.5	28.3	54.9
April 1930	89.0	48.6	54.6
April 1940	101.1	54.7	54.1
April 1950	110.5	63.5	57.4

The estimates of the labor force for 1890, 1900, 1930, and 1940 are based on those made by John D. Durand in *The Labor Force in the United States, 1890–1960*, pp. 208–209. Mr. Durand's figures are those of the census adjusted to be comparable to the 1940 census. To this adjustment I have added an adjustment (using the adjustment ratios computed by Mr. Durand, *ibid.*, p. 207) to make the figures comparable with current labor force estimates.

tions, reductions in the standard work week, the increase in paid holidays and paid vacations, and changes in managerial methods. Work places are becoming clean, bright, and cheerful; the five-day week and the paid holidays and vacations permit working to be combined with considerable leisure. Unions give workers substantial protection against arbitrary treatment by management. About one out of twelve jobs in industry is a part-time job, and the great majority of people doing part-time work prefer it to full-time work. The demand for part-time jobs will probably increase the number of such jobs in industry, and thus draw into the labor force people who do not care for full-time work. Furthermore, the drop in the standard hours of work will increase the number of persons holding two jobs — a full-time job and a part-time job. The possibility of increasing the size of the labor force by additions of women and older persons will be discussed at greater length in Chapter VI.

THE GROWING DEPENDENCE OF THE UNITED STATES UPON IMPORTED RAW MATERIALS

The United States will be more dependent upon other countries for raw materials than in the past. This dependence has been growing. The 6 per cent of the world's population that is in the United States produces and consumes about 40 per cent of the world's goods. The raw materials for this huge output must come to an increasing extent from other countries. The extraordinary technological progress of the United States will, on the whole, increase its dependence on the rest of the world for raw materials. To some extent, of course, technological progress will have the opposite effect — the development of synthetics will reduce the dependence of this country on some imported raw materials, such as wool and rubber; in general, however, the quicker the technological progress in the United States, the greater will be the need to obtain raw materials from abroad. During the next thirty years the consumption of raw materials by American industry will be greater than during the entire period from 1800 to the present. Lumber, oil, copper, lead, zinc, wool, and other raw materials will be needed and must come from abroad in increasing amounts. This growing dependence upon other countries for raw materials has profound implications for some of the country's most important problems and policies. It means that the ability of many countries to sell to the United States, and hence to buy from us, will be improved. It means also that the United States cannot afford to impose tariff barriers on scarce products, such as copper and wool.

The Continued Importance of the Replacement Demand for Capital Goods

The demand for capital goods consists of two principal parts — capital goods to increase the plant and equipment of the economy and capital goods to replace existing plant and equipment as it wears out or becomes obsolete. The first of these two demands may be called "the expansion demand" for capital goods; the second, "the replacement de-

mand." The replacement demand for capital goods is considerably larger than the expansion demand, and this pre-
ponderance of replacement demand will continue.[3] It is true,
as I shall point out in Chapter VI, that the labor force will
grow much more rapidly in the next two decades than it has
in the last two. Even the prospective large rise in the labor
force, however, will not be sufficient to make the expansion
demand for capital goods as large as the replacement demand.

As most of the demand for industrial plant and equipment continues to be replacement demand, the makers of
equipment will be encouraged to seek markets by persuading
users to discard the plant and equipment that they purchased
5, 10, 15, or 20 years ago. It is a mistake to regard competition as consisting simply of the efforts of each of a number

[3] The proportion of the current output of plant and equipment
used to increase the capital of the country has been falling for many
years and the proportion used for replacements has been rising.
Kuznets estimates that during the entire period 1869–1928 slightly
less than half of all production of plant and equipment, 46.6 per
cent, represented a net increase in plant and equipment, and 53.4
per cent represented offsets to capital consumption, that is, replacements. (Kuznets, *National Product Since 1869,* pp. 115 and 116.)
The proportion of total output of plant and equipment that represented a net increase in plant and equipment, according to his
estimates, was as follows:

1869–1878	49.6 per cent
1879–1888	57.2
1889–1898	57.9
1899–1908	54.1
1909–1918	43.1
1919–1928	36.6

of would-be sellers to persuade prospective buyers to buy from him rather than from his rivals. Competition exists also between old products now in use and new products. Many a producer of plant or equipment (or of durable consumers' goods) finds that his principal competition comes from his own output of a few years ago.

The growing importance of the replacement demand will stimulate makers of equipment to expand technological research for the purpose of improving their products and thus will tend to accelerate technological change. The efforts of makers of equipment to improve their goods will be welcome to the users, who will be led by the strong upward pressure of unions on wages to look for better and better equipment.

Basically, what is happening and will happen more than ever is the substitution of research and engineering labor for the labor used in current operations — the use of more of the former to economize the latter. This would not happen, of course, if the cost of doing research were to rise faster than the price of labor used in current operations.

The replacement demand for many durable consumer goods, such as automobiles, has long been becoming a larger part of the total demand. The replacement demand for housing has been surprisingly small. As the rate of increase in the number of families becomes smaller, the market of the housing industry will depend to a growing extent upon success in expanding the replacement demand. Unless the replacement demand can be greatly increased, the demand for houses will soon drop drastically and the housing industry will shrink in size.

A DROP IN THE LIQUIDITY OF THE ECONOMY

The economy will gradually become less liquid than it is today. One way of measuring the liquidity of the economy, as I pointed out in Chapter I, is by the ratio of liquid assets (cash, bank deposits, and government securities) to incomes and another is by the ratio of liquid assets to debts. The present high ratio of liquid assets of individuals and nonfinancial corporations to private debts will not be maintained in the long run — though it may be raised during the next two or three years by the large expenditures on rearmament. This high ratio, as I have explained in Chapter I, has been the result of the great depression and the war. The depression decreased private debts, and the war greatly increased private holdings of cash, bank deposits, and government securities. During the last several years the ratio of liquid assets to private debts has been dropping. This change has come about, not through a drop in holdings of liquid assets, but through a rise in private debts. Individuals have rapidly increased their debts in order to buy houses, durable consumer goods — things that were not available during the war. Since private debts are still abnormally low in relation to holdings of liquid assets, they are likely in the long run to grow, relative to liquid assets.

The ratio of liquid assets to incomes has been rising most of the time for generations — mainly because the money supply has grown several times faster than the national income. If people reach the conclusion that the long-term movement of prices is upward, they may become unwilling to hold larger and larger supplies of money in relation to income, and the ratio of the money supply to personal incomes and to the net national product will no longer rise.

This would be a change of great significance. A drop in the quantity of liquid assets that individuals and nonfinancial corporations were willing to hold in relation to their incomes would greatly increase the capacity of the economy to grow. It might even cause the economy to attempt to grow too rapidly, and bring about an unhealthy rise in prices and that would force the government to attempt to limit the volume of spending.

Broader Ownership of Corporate Industry

The ownership of corporate industry will become considerably broader than it is today. Although corporations produce about half of the product of American industry, they are owned, as I have pointed out in Chapter I, by little more than 6 per cent of the adult population of the country. The number of stockholders is not accurately known, but roughly 5.5 million persons own stock in corporations open to investment by the general public and more than half a million in "privately held corporations," companies not open to investment by the public. The top managements of corporations have overlooked the importance of interesting the public in owning corporate securities. Even among persons with incomes of 7500 dollars or more, only about one third are owners of corporate stock, and among persons with incomes of 5000 to 7500 dollars, the proportion is about one out of ten. Inquiries under the auspices of the Board of Governors of the Federal Reserve System indicate that the principal reason for not owning common stock is lack of familiarity. The second most common reason is that common stocks are not considered safe.[4]

Changing conditions are increasing the need for corporations to add to the number of their stockholders. Furthermore, the prospect of rising prices is likely to increase the interest of individuals in corporate stocks as an outlet for their savings. Corporations need a great increase in the number of their stockholders in order to become more completely identified with the community and to get fair treatment from the government. Millions of savers, who have been putting their money into savings banks, need investment outlets which are suitable for a period of rising prices. The stocks of strong companies are such an outlet for those savers who can afford to take appreciable risks. Others will have to invest in corporations indirectly — through investment trusts.

Of course, the majority of enterprises are not suitable investments for persons of small or moderate means. Hence

[4] The survey of consumer finances conducted under the auspices of the Board of Governors of the Federal Reserve System reports that in 1949 only 8 out of 100 spending units and in 1950 only 7 out of 100 owned stock. In addition, about half a million spending units, owned stock in privately held corporations. On the average about 1.3 persons owned stock in each spending unit that reports owning stock. (*Federal Reserve Bulletin,* October 1949, Vol. 35, p. 1190, and December 1950, Vol. 36, p. 1601.) For a definition of "spending unit" see Chapter I, Footnote 6, p. 20.

a great increase in the number of stockholders must be achieved in the main by the more well-established concerns in the more stable industries.

The acquisition of millions of new stockholders will probably require that corporations issue new types of securities. Relatively little use thus far has been made of preferred stock. And yet families of moderate incomes require a conservative investment such as a preferred stock provides. Types of participating preferred stock could be developed in order to interest preferred stockholders in the growth and success of the concern. Such types of preferred stock would also give holders some protection against a rise in the price level.

THE GROWING INFLUENCE OF STATISTICS

The economy will continue to increase and improve the collection of statistics and it will provide itself with a more complete picture of economic business conditions and trends. The collection of statistics showing conditions of life and business in the community is one of the most distinctive and important characteristics of the modern age. The United States has pioneered in gathering statistical information. Nowhere else in the world is the volume of statistical information so great and the quality, on the whole, so high — though in some countries, such as the Scandinavian countries, the vital statistics are superior to those in the United States.

Statistical information on intentions to buy are likely to

be extended and improved. Statistics on the ownership of bank deposits and on money flows are badly needed and will soon be available. Indeed, the whole field of expenditures (who buys what) is an undeveloped one. Figures on the size and distribution of income, and on the kind of people who are in the different income brackets, are still meager and will be greatly improved. Statistics on wages are notably unsatisfactory because they do not distinguish between different occupations and types of jobs so that wages in different industries can be compared. This obvious defect will be eliminated. An important undeveloped area of statistics is the field of ownership — who owns what. Before many years the country ought to be able to publish an annual balance sheet showing its principal assets and liabilities and showing what types of persons and organizations own the various classes of assets and have the various liabilities.

The development of the statistics of crime has lagged behind the development of economic and business statistics. Materials are available, however, for producing an extensive statistical series on the incidence of various types of crime and lawbreakers. The economic benefits of more adequate statistics on crime would be great. One is safe in asserting that sooner or later this important but neglected field will be cultivated.

It is hard to overestimate the importance of the growth of the collection of statistics. It changes the intellectual climate of the times — it discourages the making of reckless claims and charges, and the proposal of panaceas; it helps people see that problems have many aspects and many parts, that they must be attacked piecemeal, and that progress must be step by step. The principal charges made by Karl Marx against the capitalist system, for example, could have been shown to be untrue at the time they were made, had adequate statistical series been available. At the very time that Marx was charging capitalism with producing greater concentration of wealth, it was actually building a large middle class.

A Focused Attack upon the Problem of Low Incomes

The community will probably make an organized attack upon the problem of low incomes. This attack will transcend anything done up to now. Poverty is an ancient problem that has long been the concern of the whole community. The lack of information concerning who have low incomes, and why, has handicapped well-directed attacks upon poverty. The information that is now becoming available about the distribution of income and about the conditions of low-income recipients is taking much of the mystery out of poverty. Some of the people with low incomes have retired and have substantial amounts of property which they are gradually consuming. That, of course, is one of the proper purposes of savings — in fact, many people who have saved considerable amounts during their active years fail to consume a reasonable part of their savings during years of retirement.[5]

Other families are in the low-income group because the

[5] The annuity is a device by which people are able to consume that proportion of savings that they desire before death. It has been

chief earner is disabled and cannot work. Some disabled persons cannot be trained so that they can again do useful work, but many could have their earning power partly or entirely restored. The possibilities of rehabilitating disabled persons have thus far been very incompletely realized.

Many families have low incomes because the chief earner has retired. The number of these can be greatly reduced by raising the usual age of retirement. The community will not continue to tolerate the tendency to drop capable workers at the age of 65.

Still other families have low incomes because the chief income earner is trying to produce the wrong thing. Agriculture furnishes many examples of low incomes resulting from producing the wrong crops or too much of certain crops. In these cases the cure is a shift in occupation or a change in the goods produced.

Finally, many families lack income earners, and even potential income earners.

The availability of more or less definite information on who have low incomes will make possible a well-planned attack upon the problem of poverty. Of course, there will always be a small number in the labor force, probably about 10 per cent, who have earning capacity far below the rest of the workers — just as there is bound to be another proportion that possesses far higher earning capacity than most workers. This spread in the distribution of abilities is found regardless of the kind of ability that is being examined. There are always a few persons who possess the particular

---

used for this purpose only to a limited extent. It has great possibilities, however, as a method by which savings may be put to more effective use.

ability in very high degree and a few who possess it in very low degree.

THE GROWING DEMANDS UPON MANAGERS

The job of the business manager will become a more exacting one and will require more training. The demands made on managers by customers, by employees, by stockholders, by other members of management, and by the government have been increasing for a long time. There are no signs that these demands will become less or that the tendency to expect more of managers will cease. Employees will demand more considerate and understanding treatment and so will customers. Other members of management will expect to be treated as members of the team. One-man companies, of which there are many, will become less numerous. Stockholders will expect more of managers, and "inside deals" by which managers profit by selling things to themselves will be more severely frowned upon.[6] All of this, on the whole, is to the good. It simply

[6] The record in the past has been punctuated by such episodes as requiring a former chairman of the National City Bank of New York, Charles E. Mitchell, and associates, to repay the bank about 1.8 million dollars in bonuses paid to management; requiring the late George Washington Hill and associates to repay 2 million dollars of bonuses to the American Tobacco Company; requiring William Randolph Hearst and associates to pay Hearst Consolidated Publications, Inc. 5 million dollars because the court held that the corporation had been overcharged when it bought some of the papers from Hearst; requiring ex-Chairman C. L. Lloyd and ex-President L. Frank Pitts to repay the Nu-Enamel Corporation 1,198,000 dollars

means that the demands that a civilized society makes will press more inexorably upon management.

Management in turn may demand a higher and higher standard of conduct from trade unions, from employees, from customers, and from the government. Violations of contracts and wildcat strikes will be less tolerated. Management needs to demand far higher standards of conduct from the government — more adequate reporting of government finances, better drafting of laws by Congress, more judicial administration of laws, cessation of the efforts of administrative agencies to usurp the legislative function of Congress by putting into laws meaning that no one intended.

The reader will undoubtedly be struck by the many important topics *not* discussed in this chapter — the outlook for government intervention in economic affairs, the future of trade unions, the future position of the United States in the economy of the world, the future organization and control of the economy of the United States. All of these topics, however, involve great uncertainties, and the present chapter has been devoted to a discussion of the economic trends that seem most probable. The following chapters will discuss some important trends in areas about which there is great doubt.

---

because of company stock bought cheaply and sold to the company at a big profit. More recently there has been a challenge of the sale of properties by insiders to Textron, Inc. at excessive profits. (*Time Magazine,* May 22, 1950, p. 93.)

CHAPTER IV
Some Principal Points of Doubt about Trends in the Economy

IN THIS CHAPTER, I wish to explore some of the more uncertain aspects of the future of the economy. What, for example, is the future of small business in the United States? What will be the general nature of intervention by the government in economic affairs? Now that unions have become well established and have achieved great power, is a new type of unionism likely to develop? Are trade unions likely to sponsor a labor party in this country? What is the long-run outlook for prices? After a decade or so of rising prices, will the people eventually insist that the advance be halted?

THE FUTURE OF SMALL BUSINESS

What is the future of small business in the United States? For a long time predictions have been made that the rise of machine industry will cause small concerns to lose out in competition with large ones so that production will gradually be concentrated in fewer and fewer enterprises. Furthermore, some people seem to assume that there is some virtue in smallness as such and that a decline in the relative importance of small concerns would in itself be undesirable. It is obvious, however, that neither smallness nor bigness is a virtue or evil in itself. It is important that enterprises be fairly easy to start because this makes industry progressive and dynamic and protects it from becoming too tradition bound and custom bound. It is also important that business concerns be of the size that makes them most efficient — whether this size be large or small.

In some parts of industry, particularly manufacturing, transportation and public utilities, large concerns are dominant. Nevertheless, generally speaking, small enterprises greatly outnumber large ones. Indeed, over 98 out of 100 business concerns outside of agriculture have fewer than 50 employees. These small firms employ one third of the workers in private industry outside of agriculture. Nearly three fifths of the workers outside of agriculture are employed by enterprises that have fewer than 500 workers. Furthermore, the number of enterprises outside of agriculture has been growing faster than the population of the country. The number of concerns suffered a sharp drop during the war, but has increased rapidly since then. Today there are almost a million more concerns outside of agriculture than in 1929, and about 700,000 more than in 1945. In short, small business as a whole has been doing well.

The growth in profits, sales, and assets of small concerns compares favorably with the rise in the profits, sales, and assets of large concerns. The operating profits of all unincorporated enterprises outside of agriculture (composed almost entirely of small concerns) were 2.6 times as large in 1949 as in 1940; the operating profits of all corporations (which include, of course, all of the large concerns) were 3.1 times as large in 1949 as in 1940. Among 1000 manufacturing corporations, the sales of the 200 largest increased 100 per cent between 1939 and 1946; the sales of the 800 smallest, 148 per cent. The assets of the 200 largest increased 41 per cent between 1939 and 1946; the assets of the 800 smallest by 97 per cent.

The fact that small business has been doing well does not necessarily mean that it will continue to do so. Where markets are small and specialized, small enterprises usually have an advantage over large ones, and there will always be many small and specialized markets. In recent years there has been considerable discussion of the handicaps of small concerns in raising capital. Small enterprises do not use public issues of bonds or stocks as a means of raising capital, but this does not mean that they lack adequate sources. In the last several years, large quantities of personal savings have been invested in small concerns. During the four years 1946 to 1949 inclusive, unincorporated enterprises purchased 34.9 billion dollars of plant and equipment. Of this 18.1 billion dollars represented increases in plant and equipment of non-agricultural concerns and 16.8 billion dollars increased investment in the plant and equipment of farms.[1]

Doubts about the outlook for small business arise because of two uncertainties: first, the ability of small concerns to hold their own in competition with large and medium-sized ones as research becomes increasingly important in industry, and second, the ability of small concerns to attract

[1] In the same period nonfinancial corporations purchased 60.2 billion dollars' worth of plant and equipment.

men of ability in competition with the large. Small enterprises, as a general rule, cannot support research laboratories of their own. But there are ways by which they can get the benefit of research. Much done by the government is available for them — the research of the Department of Agriculture is an example. Small concerns, moreover, may co-operate to support research. Some concerns which cannot afford their own laboratories can get work done under contract. Finally, small concerns get the benefit of research done by large enterprises through the fact that the technology of each industry is determined to a large extent outside the industry — by the concerns that sell equipment to the industry. The coal-cutting machinery and coal-loading machines have been developed, not by the coal industry, but by machinery manufacturers; the technology of the shoe industry has been determined, not by the makers of shoes, but by the makers of shoe machinery.

Can small enterprises (or self-employment) compete successfully with well-established concerns, especially large ones, for well-qualified managers? The answer to this question is likely to be "No." Certainly at the present time the greatest lack in small concerns is not capital but well-qualified executives. The people who are best qualified to start new businesses are usually employed by well-established enterprises. Their ability and their knowledge of the industry give them bright prospects for promotion. Why should they risk going into business for themselves when they have a good chance of becoming plant managers, sales managers, or even vice presidents, and of eventually retiring on a good pension?

What is likely to be done to encourage small business?
There is political appeal in doing "something" for small
business, so something is likely to be done. It has been proposed that a unit be set up in the Department of Commerce to disseminate scientific, engineering, and managerial
information to business concerns, especially to small enterprises.[2] Such a unit, if staffed with able men, could do
much to help all firms — large and small alike — to improve their methods.

Some modifications may be made in the corporate income
tax to encourage the starting of new enterprises — and
such changes would be particularly advantageous to small
concerns, since most new enterprises are small. The most
important change would be a modification in the corporate
income tax to permit losses to be carried forward five years,
instead of two. New concerns are frequently in the "red"
for three or four years or more before they begin to make
money. When they become profitable and need to use their
earnings to expand, they become liable for taxes to the extent that their current profits have exceeded their losses
during the preceding two years. Since only a part of total
losses are offset against profits, the new concerns are in effect compelled to pay taxes out of capital.

Arrangements by which capital is made more readily
available to new and small enterprises are likely to be developed. Most of the present investment institutions, such
as commercial banks, savings banks, or insurance com-

[2] This proposal was made by Secretary Sawyer and was in-
corporated in a special message of President Truman to Congress
in May 1950.

panies, suffer from a serious handicap — they are not free to make a loan or an investment simply because it promises to be profitable. They must put the security of their depositors or their policyholders above the pursuit of profit. This limits their ability to put money into new enterprises, no matter how attractive the gamble. There is need for investment companies that are free to take any risk that seems worth taking without the necessity of protecting someone else's security. This need may be met fairly adequately by the venture-capital companies that have recently been started, such as J. H. Whitney and Company, the American Research and Development Corporation, and others.[3] Perhaps these companies will be supplemented eventually by capital banks or investment companies formed by commercial banks and insurance companies, with possibly some money from the Federal Reserve Banks.[4] The best arrangement would probably be to establish an investment company experimentally in each of two or three Federal Reserve districts with the member commercial banks and the Reserve Bank as principal stockholders. Part of the profits (if any) should be used to retire the investment of the Reserve Bank. The commercial banks would be in a position to turn over to the capital bank some business not suitable for them.

Another proposal is that the lending powers of the Reconstruction Finance Corporation be broadened to permit

[3] See Chapter I, pp. 10-11.

[4] Such capital banks were proposed by the Committee for Economic Development and later by a subcommittee of the Committee on the Economic Report of the President, by the Secretary of Commerce, Mr. Sawyer, and by President Truman.

it to relax its collateral requirements on loans to small business. This would be a mistake. The size of the borrower should not determine collateral requirements.

It remains to be seen, of course, whether enterprises that specialize on investing in risky ventures can make money. The experience of the New York Federal Reserve Bank, with 376 so-called "industrial loans" between 1934 and 1944, was that the bank roughly broke even — though the bank reports that no overhead charges were allocated to industrial loan operations.[5] Experience indicates that there are many thousands of concerns or would-be concerns that are seeking capital funds, that less than 1 per cent of these enterprises look like good gambles from the standpoint of outside investors, and that an appreciable proportion of the concerns that appear to be good gambles turn out to be bad ones. Undoubtedly experience will reduce the ratio of mistakes to the total number of investments made. Furthermore, the very existence of venture-capital companies will tend to increase the number of well-qualified persons who seek capital.

Finally, the starting of new enterprises by experienced and well-qualified business executives may be encouraged by changes in the corporate income tax to protect men who leave the service of an employer from losing the pension rights they have built up. Under the terms of nearly all private pension plans, however, an employee who leaves the service of the enterprise loses his accumulated pension rights. The corporate executive who might start a venture

[5] Federal Reserve Bank of New York, *Monthly Letter,* July 1944, pp. 51–52.

of his own is likely to have earned from five to twenty years of pension rights. The loss of these rights is a powerful deterrent to a man's starting in business for himself. The corporate income tax is likely to be amended, sooner or later, to provide that the costs of no private pension plan shall be a deductible expense under the law unless all pension rights after a minimum period of service (say one year) vest as they are earned.

These several changes — increases in the duration of the loss-carry-forward provision of the corporate income tax, the growth of venture-capital companies, changes in the corporate income tax to encourage the vesting of pension rights as they are earned — might increase by several thousand a year the well-qualified persons who start concerns of their own. Most of the enterprises started by well-qualified persons would survive, and many of them would probably grow into medium-sized or even large concerns. The effect upon the total number of business births and business deaths and the total number of enterprises in the country would, of course, be small, but the effect upon the operation of the economy would be great. Each of these new concerns, managed by a well-qualified person, would take some business away from other enterprises and would threaten to take away considerably more. Each would be compelling other enterprises to be more alert and progressive. As a result, the economy would be made more competitive and progressive. And the growth of the successful new concerns would probably raise the proportion of all business done by medium-sized enterprises.

Efforts to increase the number of well-qualified persons

who go into business for themselves would leave one important aspect of the problem of small business virtually unaffected. That is the problem of the high rate of mortality among newly started concerns. Indeed, this problem might be aggravated. The starting of several thousand additional new concerns a year by well-qualified men would not cut down the number of business deaths. In fact, it might increase them, because more well-managed new concerns would make it harder for the poorly managed ones to get business. The death rate among enterprises is high because it is fairly easy to go into business in the United States and because many Americans are ambitious and self-reliant, and have considerable confidence in themselves. Consequently, there are many poorly qualified persons going into business. The only way to cut down substantially on the number of business deaths would be to restrict drastically the freedom of people to launch ventures of their own — a remedy that no one would desire.

Although the size of business enterprises is not in itself important, it is desirable that the size be determined by the preferences of consumers and by the relative efficiency of competitors. It is particularly desirable that business concerns, regardless of their size, strive to grow larger. As soon as a concern no longer attempts to grow, the customers lose much of the benefit of competition. This is why it would be stupid to limit the proportion of business that a concern may do. The "remedy" would be as bad as the condition it seeks to prevent, namely monopoly; it would force some enterprises to behave as if they were monopolies by preventing them from competing for new business.

Many people believe that vigorous competition cannot exist unless there are a large number of rivals. As a matter of fact, the belief that concentration of a large amount of production in a few hands is bad for competition is an unsubstantiated theory about which little evidence has been assembled. The theory may be true under some conditions and not under others. Certainly the fact that the number of principal competitors is few does not discourage efforts to improve the quality of products — on the contrary, it probably intensifies such efforts. It also stimulates improvement in methods of production and thus the cutting of costs. The fact that one of several large competitors, by gaining an important advantage in costs, might greatly enlarge its market at the expense of the others, gives a powerful incentive to each of the rivals to keep abreast of the others in technological progress.

The view that the concentration of production in the hands of a few firms impairs competition in prices is based on the assumption that each large competitor will refuse to consider price cuts on the ground that its rivals will promptly meet them. This argument is true under certain conditions — it probably explains the rigidity of some prices during periods of business recessions. The argument, however, overlooks the fact that there are advantages in being first to cut prices. No one has tested whether price policies are more frequently affected by the fact that competitors would promptly meet price cuts or by the advantage of being the first to cut. Furthermore, in many industries prices have been rising during the last two decades — largely the result of higher labor costs. Where there are several large competitors, each may be reluctant to be the first to raise prices — since competitors, by refusing to meet the increases promptly, might gain many new customers. In industries where labor costs are rising, concentration of production in a few large firms may give consumers better protection against advancing prices than would the competition between many small concerns. Certainly there is no evidence to support the view that the government ought to discourage competition by limiting the size of enterprises and thus preventing large concerns from attempting to grow.

WHAT KINDS OF GOVERNMENT INTERVENTION?

What kinds of government intervention in economic affairs are most likely to grow in the future? The day may come when there may be a reversal of the trend of the last century, and when the government will reduce its intervention in economic matters. But no signs of such a reversal are yet in sight — despite such scattered instances as the repeal of the tax on oleomargarine and the reduction of many import duties. During the foreseeable future, intervention by the government is quite certain to grow. The following are some of the kinds of government intervention that seem most probable.

1. *Public works for the purpose of developing and conserving resources and improving transportation.* As the population of the country increases and as the consumption of raw materials rapidly rises, the demand that the govern-

ment provide water and water power and that it protect established communities against floods and polluted streams will grow stronger. The steady increase in the number of automobiles and trucks will force the government to spend much larger amounts on highways — although, as I have pointed out in Chapter III, there is a great opportunity to provide important investment opportunities by constructing many of the needed highways as toll roads, thus relieving taxpayers in part from the burden of providing free highways. In the older cities of the country, the necessity for clearing slums will put the government in the housing business on a growing scale. In short, public works are bound to be stimulated by the fact that the United States is becoming a more crowded country and is using its limited resources very swiftly.

2. *Measures to limit fluctuations in business.* Although, as we have seen, the economy has gained considerably in stability, additional measures to promote this are likely to be adopted. The temporary authority that the Federal Reserve System now has to control the terms of consumer credit will probably be allowed to expire when the present defense emergency is over. But unless the Reserve System is sooner or later given permanent authority to fix the terms of consumer credit, the volume of such credit will gradually expand to such high levels that the repayment of loans will seriously aggravate periods of deflation. Arrangements for controlling the expansion of commercial credit are unsatisfactory and sooner or later something will probably be done about them. Just what will be done is not clear. An obvious way to control lending by the com-

mercial banks is to limit the size of their reserves through the sale of government securities by the Federal Reserve Banks. But such sales depress the price of government bonds. With the Federal debt large and with the government frequently in need of borrowing, many people believe that government bonds should not be permitted to fall below par. Consequently, bond sales by the Federal Reserve Banks may be little used to limit lending by commercial banks.

Another way by which bank credit might be controlled is by granting authority to the Reserve System to require higher reserves against increases in bank deposits than are required against outstanding deposits. Such authority would permit the Reserve Banks to impose very strong obstacles to further expansion of bank credit without forcing the banks to curtail outstanding loans.[6]

3. *Measures to increase the proportion of income distributed on the basis of need*. In the previous chapter I pointed out that the present Federal pension plan will undoubtedly be extended to cover most of the self-employed who are now excluded and that some form of sickness and disability insurance seems inevitable. The many sickness and disability plans negotiated between unions and employers are limited to plants in which unions are recognized and none of them apply to the self-employed. There is a possibility, however,

---

[6] The Reserve Banks now possess authority to raise the reserves required by member banks against *all* deposits. Increases in reserves against all deposits is such a powerful instrument that it is likely to produce more curtailment of credit than would be desirable. Hence it is rarely used by the Reserve System.

that the spread of private plans negotiated by trade unions will so weaken the demand for a government plan that such a plan will not be provided.

4. *Intervention in the field of industrial relations.* Further intervention in the field of industrial relations is probable — though many union leaders and many employers do not like it. The great growth of unions and the prevalence of the union shop make the right to belong to a union and the administration of discipline by unions of increasing importance to employees. There are many important industries in which a man cannot obtain or hold a job unless he is a member in good standing of the union that holds the bargaining rights. And yet there are some unions, including the important railroad brotherhoods, that will not admit Negroes, and there is an appreciable minority of unions that impose very high initiation fees. It is obviously intolerable that exclusive bargaining rights be given to organizations that do not maintain an open door on reasonable terms. Indeed, the present administration of the Railway Labor Act is probably unconstitutional because exclusive bargaining rights are conferred on unions that exclude men because of color. The orders conferring exclusive jurisdiction under these circumstances violate the Fifth Amendment.

No less important than the right to join a union is the right to remain in one. There are a number of unions, however, that permit men to be disciplined for such vague offenses as slandering an officer, creating dissension, undermining the union or working against its interest, action which is dishonorable or which might injure the labor movement.[7] The way in which disciplinary cases are handled is unsatisfactory in many unions. Most of them, for example, do not permit members in a closed shop or a union shop who appeal from disciplinary action by the union to hold their jobs pending appeal if the penalty imposed on the man was suspension or expulsion from the union. If the discipline is a fine, the member usually is required to pay it or a substantial part of it in order to appeal his case.[8] In view of the importance that unions have attained in the economy, the government may be expected to protect the right to belong to a union and to protect the rights of union members. An important beginning has been made by some states, such as New York and Massachusetts, which forbid unions from excluding persons on the ground of race, color, or creed. Massachusetts also provides protection from arbitrary discipline of members by unions. It forbids union members who have had discipline imposed on them by the union from being deprived of the right to work while appealing their cases within the union. It also provides an appeal from the highest authority within the union to the State Labor Relations Board, which may set aside the union

[7] An examination of the constitutions of 81 unions showed the several offenses made punishable as follows: slandering an officer, 29 unions; creating dissension, 15 unions; undermining the union or working against its interest, 20 unions; action which is dishonorable or which might injure the labor movement, 25 unions. (Philip Taft, "Judicial Procedure in Labor Unions," *Quarterly Journal of Economics,* May 1945, pp. 370–385.)

[8] Philip Taft, "Status of Members in Unions During Appeal from Penalty Imposed by the Local Union," *Quarterly Journal of Economics,* August 1948, Vol. 62, pp. 610–616.

decision in case it finds that the member did not have a fair trial, that he was disciplined on grounds contrary to public policy (such as campaigning against the union's political program), or that the discipline was too drastic for the offense. Some regulations of unions should be uniform throughout the several states, and should be handled by the Federal government rather than by the states. An example is the regulation of admission requirements, including admission fees.

Some of the proposals to regulate the internal affairs of unions have been foolish and have been made by persons who are hostile to unions and who wish to stir up public opinion against them. An example of a foolish regulation is the proposal that unions be required to elect officers every year. Certainly there is nothing wrong with a two-year, three-year, or four-year term. In fact, a longer term permits the officers to place emphasis upon policies that do not yield results immediately and to take account of the long-run effects of all policies. Furthermore, it relieves the officers of the necessity of running for office continuously and enables them to devote more time to the affairs of the union.

The government will need to limit the scope of industrial conflict and protect neutrals from being forced to help the union members or the employer in a conflict. The government has been lax in permitting strikes, lockouts, and boycotts to be used for unjustifiable purposes — such as to force men to join a particular union, to force the employer to assign work to members of a given union, or to cease dealing with certain enterprises. The common law on the rights of neutrals is indefinite and confused, and suitable means of enforcing it are lacking. A crude attempt was made in the Taft-Hartley Act to give protection to neutrals, but this Act is quite inadequate.

Methods of dealing with stoppages that imperil the public health or the public safety or that threaten economic disaster must be developed. There are now a considerable number of industries in which a stoppage of work would imperil the health or safety of the country or the population of a community or would inflict economic disaster upon the country. A nation-wide shutdown of railroad transportation would soon create a national emergency. So also would a nation-wide shutdown of coal or steel production, if it continued for many weeks. The shutdown of electric-power plants, water works, or gasworks, or the stoppage of the delivery of food and fuel, would create an emergency in most communities.

It is inevitable that special duties be imposed on unions and employers when their failure to settle their differences would imperil public health or public safety or, indeed, inflict severe economic loss on the country. There has been considerable experimental legislation by the Federal government and the states. Much of it has been bad because it has discouraged employers and unions from settling their differences by negotiation or arbitration. The Railway Labor Act is an example. This law provides that if stoppage of work on the railroads (or other companies covered by the Act) threatens to create a national emergency, the President may appoint an emergency board which will recommend a settlement. Acceptance of the recommendations of the emergency board is not required but a stoppage may not occur until thirty days after the board has made its report public. The opportunity to get disputes before emergency boards has seriously impaired the willingness of the railroad unions to bargain with the railroads or to submit their disputes to arbitration. Furthermore, in recent years almost all of the reports of emergency boards have been rejected by the unions. In several cases the rejection of the emergency board reports has led to seizure of the roads by the government; in other cases, it has led the President to intervene in the dispute as a mediator or arbitrator.

Unions appear to prefer to bargain with the roads seized by the government or with the President as a mediator. If the President were authorized to require the two sides to put into effect the recommendations of an emergency board for a limited period (say six months or nine months), and if the government, on seizing the roads, were required either to maintain existing wages and working conditions or to put into effect the recommendations of the emergency board and were expressly forbidden to enter into agreements with the unions that would establish wages or working conditions different from either the existing conditions or those recommended by the emergency boards, the attractiveness of emergency boards to both unions and employers would be greatly reduced and the two sides would be given a powerful incentive to settle their disputes by negotiation or arbitration.

5. *Intervention to control or assist a rise in prices or to limit the wage increases that are negotiated under collective bargaining.* Unions are probably strong enough, as I have pointed out, to raise wages faster than the managers and

engineers can raise physical output per man-hour. Hence labor costs will rise. Perhaps prices will increase even faster than wages — either because of the tremendous defense orders of the government or because consumers, expecting that rising wages will force higher prices, will buy in anticipation of price advances. At any rate, if prices rise over the long term, as seems likely, the question of what to do about this will become of great importance and also highly controversial. (This matter will be discussed more fully in the last section of this chapter.)

6. *Regulation of the pricing practices and policies of business.* The government already imposes many price ceilings and price floors, and, through interpretations of the Sherman Act and the Clayton Act and through the Robinson-Putnam Act, it undertakes to regulate price cutting, price discrimination, and other pricing practices. Many of the states have price-maintenance laws designed to discourage price cutting by retailers. The demand for still further regulation of pricing practices and policies is strong, particularly among some groups of businessmen, such as small manufacturers, producers of trade-marked goods, and independent retailers. Hence, it seems likely to spread.

The prospective spread of government regulation of pricing practices and policies is regrettable. Much of the intervention in this field has been contrary to the national interest because it has been designed to protect business concerns (especially small concerns) from vigorous competition rather than to give consumers the benefit of competition. In short, it has tended to make the economy less competitive, less efficient, and less progressive. For example, the Department of Justice has successfully contended that cutting prices for the purpose of increasing the volume of business and thereby reducing costs is a violation of the Sherman Act — although such behavior is normal when unit costs drop as production increases, and although it helps in getting production concentrated in the most efficient enterprises.[9] Furthermore, the government has prohibited price discrimination in selling to different buyers at different prices, although attempts of buyers to obtain more favorable bargains and of sellers to gain customers by making special concessions undoubtedly make competition more vigorous. In the A and P case, the government successfully contended that it was illegal for the A and P Company to win for itself the largest possible concession because it bought directly from food processors and packers instead of buying through the brokers.

Government intervention in the field of pricing practices and policies is being developed without adequate investigation of the problems involved, without adequate consideration of the consequences of the proposed interpretation of the antitrust laws, and without a clear conception of the proper objectives of national policy. Hence, this part of the antitrust policy of the government is a serious threat to the future efficiency of the economy.

7. *Regulation of the structure of industry.* In recent years some government agencies and some courts have developed

[9] The case holding such practices to be illegal is *U.S.* v. *The New York Great A and P Tea Co.,* 67 Fed. Supp. 626. An illuminating discussion of the case by Mr. A. Adelman appears in the *Quarterly Journal of Economics,* May 1949, Vol. LXIII, pp. 238–257.

the view that the integration of industry (the combination of several stages of production, such as manufacturing and retailing, under one ownership) may under some circumstances be a restraint of trade. Some companies, such as the Pullman Company and the Paramount Studios, have been required or induced to divide themselves into separate enterprises. In the A and P case, the government asked that the A and P Company divest itself of its manufacturing operations because it could manufacture some products cheaper than it could buy them, and thus undersell its competitors.[10] It remains to be seen whether the government will attempt, through the antitrust laws, to control the structure of American industry.

Such an attempt would be most unfortunate. It is, of course, true that the ways in which trade may be unlawfully restrained are innumerable and that practices and arrangements, lawful in themselves, may be part of an unlawful scheme. Hence, one cannot argue that a given arrangement, such as an integrated company, may never under *any* circumstances be a device for restraining trade. But the mere fact that integration increased the efficiency of the company and thereby enabled it to win trade away from rival companies (thereby restraining their trade) would not make it a violation of law. That is the kind of restraint of trade (taking business away from rivals) that the Sherman Act is intended to *encourage*. Nor should the fact that integration increases the bargaining power of a

[10] The government brief described this as "an inherent abuse of the vertical integration of A and P's System." (Quoted by Adelman in *Quarterly Journal of Economics*, Vol. LXIII, p. 244.)

buyer, enabling him to undersell his rivals unless they improve their efficiency and reduce their costs, make it an illegal restraint of trade. The process of driving down prices and of underselling competitors is what the antitrust laws are intended to protect and encourage.

The present decisions on integration and restraint of trade provide no rule by which any enterprise can determine whether or not it is violating the law and they reveal no clear conception of the purpose of the antitrust laws. In fact, the prosecutions and decisions reveal confusion in the Department of Justice and the courts — failure to distinguish between protecting enterprises from stiff competition and protecting consumers from lack of stiff competition. Managements should obviously be free to adopt any degree of integration that makes for efficiency. The judgment of one management on this point may well differ from the judgment of another management. The judgment of these managements ten years hence may be very different from their judgment today. They should be free to experiment — in fact, they should be *encouraged* to experiment.

The danger of rigid separation of economic functions such as the government now seeks to encourage is illustrated by the construction industry, where such separation exists, preventing manufacturers from dealing directly with users and giving material men a profit on all material going from manufacturers to users. Most manufacturers fear to challenge this uneconomic arrangement because such a challenge would cause them to be boycotted by material dealers.

Another illustration of uneconomic separation of functions is provided by the British cotton industry where spinning and weaving (contrary to American practice) are done by separate enterprises. The London *Economist* reporting on the recent visit of three productivity teams from the British cotton textile industry to the United States says:

"All the American mills visited were vertically integrated concerns that did their own spinning. Their high output per man derived from automatic machines, efficiently utilized; the machines were devised, and their operation planned, on the assumption that supplies of yarn of a high and regular standard of weavability could be assured. 'Weavability' is not the same as 'quality' in the ordinary sense; it means, substantially, freedom from loom breakages on the machines for which the yarn is spun. Thus, when the visiting team saw pillow cottons being woven at more than 90 per cent efficiency and 104 looms per weave, it saw something that could not conceivably be attained in the 'characteristic' British weaving concern, which is horizontally organized and therefore does not control its own supply of yarn.

"In the particular sample given, the report concedes that 'few firms in Britain could weave such cloths at more than eight non-automatic looms and 85 per cent efficiency.' " [11]

The purpose of these illustrations is not to argue that integration is normally superior to separation of functions, because there is no general rule. The purpose is to show that separation of functions easily becomes established and that integration is not readily established, even though it would be more efficient. The conclusion is that

[11] *Economist,* July 1, 1950, p. 34.

public policy should be neutral on the matter of integration versus separation of functions and that the decision should be left to management.

Although attempts to regulate the structure of industry by law would prevent useful experimentation by managements with different kinds of structure, would limit efficiency, and would discourage competition, there is a demand for it from some business groups that wish to convert the antitrust laws from acts designed to protect consumers from monopoly into acts protecting business concerns from stiff competition. The consumers are unorganized and inarticulate. Perhaps their interest will win out, but the prospect is uncertain.

8. *Regulation of the degree of concentration of industry.* Some government agencies believe that the success of an enterprise in gaining a high proportion of business in an industry is a violation of the antitrust laws. Restrictions on bigness have a strong popular appeal. Consequently, the government may attempt to impose limits on the proportion of business that an enterprise may do.

If the courts can be persuaded to accept the view that winning a high proportion of business violates the antitrust laws or if Congress can be induced to set limits on the percentage of business in an industry that a concern may do, an important extension of government control over industry will have been accomplished. Furthermore, the economy will have been made less competitive and less dynamic.

I have pointed out in the previous section that legal limits on the proportion of business that an enterprise may do would compel some concerns to behave like monopolies —

no matter how far from being monopolies they might be. They would be compelled to be interested in making money by charging a higher price rather than by increasing their sales. If concerns are to be broken up because they do too large a share of the business, it should be only those concerns that are behaving monopolistically by not attempting to grow at the expense of rivals. There is no reason to break up enterprises that are behaving as good competitors should behave — namely, attempting to grow faster than the rest of the industry.

Although the government should not ordinarily undertake to regulate the proportion of business done by any concern, the managements of large enterprises should consider from time to time whether efficiency and administrative advantages would not be gained by dividing up the concern into two, three, or four parts or more. In many cases (perhaps in most cases) such division would not be advantageous. On the other hand, it would be surprising if there were *no* cases in which enterprises, for one reason or another, have grown too large for the greatest efficiency. In such cases, the interests of the stockholders and the community alike would be served by dividing up the concern. Many enterprises have more or less unrelated operations and could easily be divided.

It is noteworthy that the voluntary division of an enterprise almost never occurs. This suggests that there is a bias on the part of top management against dividing up concerns — perhaps because the higher-ups prefer to be the heads of very large corporations rather than the heads of smaller concerns. If the division of enterprises is prevented by a managerial bias against this sort of thing, it is quite probable that a considerable number of concerns are now uneconomically large.

How Will Trade Unions Develop?

Now that trade unions have become strong and pervasive, will a new type of unionism develop in the United States, different in its objectives, policies, and methods from the "business unionism" that has been primarily concerned with wages, hours, and shop rules? Have the objectives and methods of unions been largely a result of the newness of unions, of their limited membership, of the weakness of many unions, and of their limited influence in the community? Now that unions have a large membership, great strength, and great influence, are not their objectives bound to become broader and more ambitious? Are they likely to be more interested in the state of the nation as a whole, or at least the state of wage earners as a whole? Are they likely to rely to an increasing extent upon political action to achieve their objectives? May not unions be expected even to sponsor the organization of a labor party, as unions in some other countries have done?

My belief is that the growth in the experience, membership, strength, and influence of unions will make surprisingly little difference in their objectives. There will, however, be important changes in the policies and methods of unions — mainly through the addition of new policies or methods or increased emphasis upon certain ones, rather than through the abandonment of the old. Unions will not

sponsor an independent labor party, and while their influence in the established political parties will be great, it
will also be limited. Unions will not be able to "take over"
either the Democratic or the Republican Party.

The reason that the objectives of unions will not change
is that unions are designed to be bargaining organizations.
This means that they are poorly adapted to the pursuit of
other objectives — such as promoting the welfare of all
workers or the general welfare of the community. Each
national union is limited in membership to an occupation
or a few occupations or to an industry or a few industries —
that is, to groups of workers who have common economic
interests.[12] The membership of unions is both too *in*clusive
and too *ex*clusive to make them well adapted for promoting the welfare of all workers and particularly for political
action. The membership is too inclusive because unions,
in order to do a good job of bargaining, must usually admit
all workers in the groups they represent, regardless of the
views of these workers upon social or political issues. For
example, a union that seeks to bargain effectively for the
carpenters must admit all carpenters, whether they are

[12] There are a few unions that contain workers of more or less
different economic interests. There is no close connection, for example, between the economic interests of the workers employed by
electric light and power companies and the electrical workers in
the building trades or the workers employed in factories producing
electrical goods. And yet all of these workers belong to one A.F.
of L. union. District 50 of the United Mine Workers is an organization that includes workers from a wide variety of occupations or
industries. In general, however, unions are limited to groups that
have common economic interests.

Republicans, Democrats, or Socialists. Likewise, unions cannot weaken their solidarity and introduce dissension into their ranks by taking positions on political issues that have nothing to do with bargaining. Nor will unions in bargaining refrain from pressing stiff demands in order to avoid jeopardizing the election chances of labor-supported candidates.

The membership of unions is too exclusive for the pursuit of the welfare of all workers or of the general welfare of the community because even the largest unions contain only about a million members. This is such a small part of the labor force that even these large unions cannot afford to take account of the effect of their policies upon employees as a whole or the community as a whole. It is true that most of the national unions are banded together into great federations. There are over a hundred of them in the American Federation of Labor, which has about 8 million members; and about 40 of them in the Congress of Industrial Organizations, which has about 4 million members. These federations might seem to be large enough to interest themselves in the welfare of employees as a whole, which might well happen if it were not for the fact that the two federations are controlled by their member national unions; they do not control the national unions. One of the main purposes of the national unions that established the American Federation of Labor was to protect their autonomy. In organizing the A.F. of L. the national unions were careful to create a servant, not a boss. The delegates to the conventions of both the A.F. of L. and the C.I.O. are pretty largely controlled by the officers of the various national unions — and, in fact, are in the main the officers of the national unions. The executive council of each organization consists of officers of the national unions.

All of this indicates why bargaining and the pursuit of policies designed to promote the welfare of the entire working class or of the community do not mix, and why unions are not likely to change their objectives. But unions may be expected to change their methods and policies mainly by adding new ones.

A few unions will become interested in helping employers increase output, and most unions will pay much more attention to politics of the pressure-group sort. Strong unions will be able to convert increases in productivity into higher wages. It is not probable, however, that they will cooperate with management to increase output except in high-cost plants where the employer is barely holding his own in competition. When an enterprise has low costs and is profitable, it will not be easy to persuade union members to help the employer make more money. And under those conditions management is not likely to desire the help of the union.

Unions may be expected to increase their interest in politics of the pressure-group sort, partly to influence the ways in which the government regulates their activities and partly to supplement their traditional bargaining methods. Most of the proposals to regulate unions are opposed by the officers of unions and by a substantial part of the membership.[13] As unions grow larger and stronger, the demands

[13] There is evidence that a large proportion of union members regard some type of regulation as desirable. In the fall of 1946, for

for regulation of their affairs will become more insistent. Members therefore will be stimulated to become more active as a political-pressure group. Furthermore, as the government intervenes more and more in the settlement of industrial disputes, unions will find it more and more advantageous to be able, directly or indirectly, to affect the decisions of administrative officers, and to influence the selection of administrators and members of fact-finding and arbitration boards. Certain laws, such as those prescribing minimum wages and maximum hours in plants of government contractors, or regulating wages and hours throughout industry in general, and social security laws, are of special interest to unions. When unions were weak, they were afraid to support minimum wage legislation or social security legislation lest such laws would encourage their members to rely for better conditions upon legislation rather than on collective bargaining. Now that unions are well-established and strong, they do not fear that social legislation will weaken the interest of their members in their unions. Hence they now support proposals to raise legal minimum wages and to liberalize and extend social insurance.

Although the present strength of unions undoubtedly increases their interest in labor legislation, it was the great depression, not the growth of union strength, that caused the A.F. of L. to abandon its traditional policy of opposition to social insurance. In 1930 at Boston and in 1931 at

example, the industrial state of Massachusetts overwhelmingly adopted a proposal to require unions to make financial reports. Even in many labor wards the majority in favor of the proposal was large.

Vancouver, the A.F. of L. issued strong declarations *against* unemployment insurance. But, as unemployment became worse and relief for the idle less adequate, the Federation could no longer oppose unemployment insurance. Consequently, in 1932 at Cincinnati, it endorsed such a measure — subject to the condition that insurance be established by the states, and that a national scheme be avoided.

Many people believe that the large membership and great power of the trade unions will cause them to form and sponsor a labor party. These persons believe that such a party is a logical complement of trade unions. Most other industrial countries have developed labor parties of some kind. Since four out of five workers in the United States are employees, is not a labor party here inevitable? I do not believe that a labor party is inevitable here, and I do not expect that unions will help establish one. There are three principal reasons for this belief.

One is the fact that, even though most workers are employees, they are also keenly interested in many issues that do not directly concern them as employees — foreign policy, tax policy, tariff policy, and agricultural policy. Employees in the United States are not a submerged class or an isolated part of the community that are led by bad conditions to place their interests as employees above their interests in these other matters. Hence, in order to win elections, a political party must have a program that goes beyond the matters that primarily concern union members — the government's regulation of industrial relations, its handling of strikes, its policy toward wages and hours, its social security policy. On these non-labor issues, such as foreign policy or taxation, employees are divided about as much as the rest of the community. Hence a party that limited its attention to matters of particular concern to union members would not win many votes, and a party that took a position on enough issues to win elections would divide the labor vote. Consequently, the United States will not have a labor party of the European type.

A second reason for believing that unions will not undertake to establish a labor party in the United States is that the experience of other countries shows that the rise of a labor party would transfer the leadership of the labor movement from the hands of unions to the leaders of that party. The reason for this is fairly obvious. A party, in order to win votes, must undertake to make public its policy on all important national problems. Hence the views of its leaders are bound to command greater public interest than the views of men who are heads of different unions — than the heads of the carpenters' union, the teamsters' union, or the miners' union. In England men have advanced from the leadership of important unions to membership in the Cabinet, but there have been no instances of "advancement" from positions high in the Labour Party to the leadership of unions. The British trade unionists who sponsored the Labour Party two generations ago did not have this experience to guide them. American trade union leaders, benefiting by the experience of recent years, will be more averse than ever to sponsoring any labor party.

A third reason why American unions will not establish such a party is that unions are learning that great economic power is a handicap to political influence. Big business learned this some time ago. So long as unions were the underdogs, their endorsements were often of considerable help to a candidate. In many districts the endorsement of organized labor is still a help. But as people see more clearly the huge economic power possessed by unions, the public will be more and more reluctant to support candidates who are regarded as subservient to unions and will be more inclined to support candidates who are independent and perhaps even opposed by unions because of their independence.

The failure of trade unions to acquire great political power will not mean that the United States is not a laboristic society — that is, a society in which employees are the most influential group in the community and in which laws, policies, and institutions largely reflect the interests of employees. The interests and views of employees are only imperfectly reflected in organizations that are as limited in size and as specialized in purpose as are trade unions.

THE LONG-RUN OUTLOOK FOR PRICES

In the previous chapter, I asserted that the movement of prices during most of the next decade would be slowly upward. But will this creeping increase in prices continue indefinitely? Is it not bound sooner or later to be converted into a galloping increase that soon ends in a great collapse? And if this does happen, will not the public sooner or later revolt against the advance in prices and insist that the government do something to stop it?

If people once believed that the long-run movement of

prices would be upward, many thousands of individuals and business concerns might attempt to convert a large part of their holdings of money and bonds into commodities, stocks, or real estate; this would bring about a galloping rise in prices. But whether or not this will occur depends upon how the actual rate of increase in prices affects expectations of price increases and upon how expectations in turn affect the actual rate of price increase.

There are several possibilities. If a given advance in the price level produces the belief that prices will continue to rise at that rate and if this expectation causes the actual increase in prices to exceed the expected increase, a creeping rise in prices will obviously soon be converted into a galloping rise. Consider, for example, the possibility that an actual rise of 3 per cent per year in prices created the expectation that this 3 per cent rate of increase would continue and that this expectation led people to buy goods in such quantities that the actual rise in prices was 4 per cent. The conditions for a galloping rise in prices are evidently present, because the actual rise of 4 per cent would soon create the expectation of a 4 per cent rise and this, in turn, would cause the actual rise soon to become greater than 4 per cent.

Quite different, however, would be the situation if expectations of rising prices should cause only a limited amount of forward buying. The rate at which prices advanced might then be raised by expectations up to a certain point, but not beyond it.

Undoubtedly there is some critical rate of increase in the price level that will cause millions of persons to decide to reduce substantially their holdings of cash and fixed dollar assets and to buy commodities, real estate or stocks. If the advance in prices were to exceed this critical rate, and if nothing were done to restrain it, the rise would become faster and faster and end in collapse. But undoubtedly steps would be taken in the form of credit control to halt the cumulative increase in prices.

Much more likely is the prospect that the expectation of price increases will raise the actual increase in prices by a limited amount, but by no more than this limited amount. There are several reasons for this belief. The prospect of a slow general rise in prices does not, of course, mean that the price of any particular commodity or article will advance. Hence the expectation of a slow rise in the average level of *all* prices may not be particularly effective in stimulating individuals or business concerns to buy any *specific* articles in anticipation of higher prices. The possibility of improvements in some goods will also deter advance buying. A drop in the price of bonds and a rise in the price of equities and real estate would discourage the tendency to shift from bonds into real estate and equities. Finally, purchases by each individual and enterprise would also be limited by uncertainties concerning the size of future incomes, by the possibility of unemployment or the loss of markets, and by the necessity of going into debt.

But will the public tolerate even a slow rise in prices? Such a creeping increase in prices works a grave injustice upon many parts of the community. It is, of course, equivalent to a creeping expropriation of certain types of property such as bonds and savings deposits. At the end of 1949, individuals owned nearly 53 billion dollars of savings deposits, over 41 billion of United States government securities, and 11.6 billion of savings and loan shares.[14] If prices were to rise 33 per cent in 10 years, the owners of such property would in effect be deprived of one third of their savings deposits, holdings of government bonds, and holdings of savings and loan shares.

After the slow increase in prices has been going on for some years, the public may therefore revolt against it and demand that steps be taken to halt it. Such steps could not succeed, however, as long as trade unions were strong enough to push up wages faster than managements were able to raise physical output per man-hour. It has been suggested that rising wages might be controlled through a national wage policy formulated and operated by the federations of unions — the A.F. of L. and the C.I.O. or a body representing both. The unions might estimate how much increase in production there would be each year to be converted into higher wages, and might undertake to decide how much each union should have. Such a policy would prevent a few strong unions from getting most of the possible rise in real wages. In Britain a policy of wage restraint was operated by the unions for several years. The British unions, however, have acted only in the face of a clear and grave national emergency and in response to an appeal from the labor government. Furthermore, in the summer of 1950, when the Korean war and rearmament made the need for restraint greater than ever, the unions abandoned the pol-

[14] This does not include the quantities of these assets held in trust funds of which individuals were the beneficiaries.

icy.[15] The tradition of autonomy among the unions is stronger in the United States than in Britain, and the influence of the A.F. of L. and the C.I.O. with their constituent unions is less than the influence of the British Trade Union Council.[16] Consequently, the chance that a policy of wage restraint might be operated by unions in the United States is quite remote.

If the tendency for rising wages to push up prices cannot

[15] It was proposed that the Trade Union Council act as arbiter among the unions in determining priorities of wage claims. (*Economist,* May 27, 1950, p. 1159.)

[16] As a matter of fact, as I pointed out in the previous section, the men who make policy in both the A.F. of L. and the C.I.O. are the heads of powerful national unions and each federation is intended to serve the national unions, not to control them. It is a mistake to regard either the A.F. of L. or the C.I.O. as an organization that is able to represent the interests that its members have in common when those interests conflict with the interests of the members of particular unions.

Within the national unions the policy-making officers and executive officers of most British unions are more independent of political pressure from the members than are the officers of national unions in the United States. The policy-making in most British unions is done by the national executive council which is composed of nonsalaried officers who hold jobs in the shops. Hence, their livelihood does not depend upon their success in winning and holding the approval of the rank and file. The full-time executive officers, who carry out policies (and on whom the policy-makers lean heavily for advice), usually hold office for life. In most American unions, on the other hand, policies are both made and executed by full-time officers who come up for re-election at frequent intervals. Hence, they are far more sensitive than the officers of British unions to the immediate desires of the members.

be controlled by the trade unions themselves, the country may decide to regulate the process of collective bargaining. It is plain that the people who set the wages of a country fundamentally determine its price level because in the long run prices must adjust themselves to labor costs. Setting wages by collective bargaining transfers the determination of the price level to numerous bargaining groups, each of which is too small to be much interested in how its bargain affects the community as a whole. The country may decide that it cannot permit its price level to be determined in this way.

Nothing less than the integrity of the dollar is at stake, because people cannot afford to hold, over a long period of time, assets payable in a fixed number of dollars if the value of the dollar steadily drops. The community may be forced to choose, therefore, between subjecting collective bargaining to fairly drastic control and accepting a dollar that does not command confidence because it is expected to fall in value. That will be a hard choice. Nevertheless, it looks as if the country will eventually have to decide which alternative is the lesser evil — the regulation of collective bargaining or the acceptance of a steadily depreciating dollar.

CHAPTER V

The Position of the United States in the World Economy

THE ECONOMIC POSITION OF THE UNITED STATES

IN A WORLD where poverty is the rule, the United States is conspicuous for its high rate of productivity and its high standard of living. The 6 per cent of the world's population living here produces and consumes about 40 per cent of the current output of the world. This means that about 40 per cent of the world's markets are in the United States. It also means that the average worker in the United States is about ten times as productive as the average worker in the rest of the world. There are a few other countries, such as Canada, Australia, and New Zealand, where labor is just about as productive as in the United States, and there are many others, such as Britain, Sweden, Denmark, where labor is more than half as productive as in the United States. Russia, with 25 per cent more people than the United States, produces less than one third as much product. It is not ordinarily appreciated what a large part of the world's population lives in extreme poverty. Just before the beginning of the Second World War, about 65 per cent of the people in the world lived in countries with an annual income of less than 100 dollars per capita and more than four fifths of the world's population lived in countries with an annual per capita income of 200 dollars or less.[1]

The sales of the rest of the world to the United States and its purchases from this country are a large part of all trade between countries. For example, in 1949, merchandise imports into this country were 12 per cent of world imports, and exports from here 21 per cent of all exports.[2] Although the exports and imports of the United States are important in world trade, they are small in relation to domestic economic activity, and during the last century this ratio has been slowly getting smaller. Imports of goods and services into the United States in 1949 were only about 4.1 per cent of the net national product, and exports were only 6.7 per cent.[3] Merchandise imports alone (exclusive

[1] U.S. Department of State, *Point Four*, pp. 113–114.

[2] *Federal Reserve Bulletin*, August 1950, Vol. 36, p. 970. In 1938, the ratios were smaller — merchandise imports into the United States were 8.9 per cent of total world imports and exports were 14.1 per cent. But in 1938 the ratio of merchandise imports to the commodity purchases by individuals and business was the same as in 1949 — 5.3 per cent.

[3] Imports of goods and services in 1949 were 9.7 billion dollars, exports were 16.0 billion dollars, and the net national product was 236.8 billion dollars. (*Federal Reserve Bulletin*, August 1950, Vol. 36, p. 970; and *Survey of Current Business*, July 1950, Vol. 30, p. 10.) Services are "imported" when Americans use the services of foreign steamship companies, airlines, insurance companies, or banks, or when they travel abroad.

of services) were about 5.3 per cent as large as all purchases of commodities by individuals and business.[4] Over a hundred years ago imports were nearly 10 per cent of the national product. Many important countries are far more dependent upon foreign trade both for goods to consume and for markets than is the United States. For example, Britain, Canada, Sweden, and the Netherlands are dependent upon imports for about one third of their standard of living, and France and Australia for about one sixth.

The rich and successful economy of the United States is under attack by Russia and other countries that would like to destroy our political and economic institutions and replace them with Communism. The attack of the Communists, of course, is not only against the United States — Russia is seeking to establish Communism in every country in the world. Her greatest efforts are directed against countries in which the standard of living is low, governments are inefficient and corrupt, and there is little local capital or managerial skill to introduce up-to-date methods of production. In such countries the Communists hold out glowing pictures of the rise in the standard of living that they will bring about. For example, the Malayan Communist Party proposes a "People's Democratic Republic" that will confiscate all British and "imperialist capital," will replace

[4] Individuals and business purchased 141.9 billion dollars of commodities in 1949. This excludes construction and services and does not include the purchase of commodities by the government. (*Survey of Current Business,* July 1950, Vol. 30, p. 9.) Merchandise imports in 1949 were 7.5 billion dollars. (*Federal Reserve Bulletin,* August 1950, Vol. 36, p. 970.)

"extortionate" taxes by "reasonable and light simple taxes," will provide equal rights for all races, higher minimum wages, free and universal elementary education, free hospitals and sanatoria for the aged, many new technical schools and universities, and the ownership of land by the peasants.[5]

In some countries Russia fosters aspirations of national independence and sees to it that the most vigorous advocates of nationalism are also Communists. But although the most active *immediate* efforts to establish Communism are being made in Asia and Europe, there can be no doubt that Russia regards the United States as her greatest and most formidable enemy. From this country comes the strongest opposition to her efforts to introduce Communism into other countries. Consequently, Russia is seeking to turn the world against the United States. She is aided in this in some parts of the world, especially Asia, by the revolt against the West and "colonialism." Indeed, many leaders of non-Communist countries regard economic relations with the United States as dangerous. They are afraid that we are attempting to dominate their lives and their economies. For example, at the British Commonwealth Conference on economic aid to South and Southeast Asia at Sidney in May 1950, the representative of Nehru argued that economic infiltration by the West, not Communism, was the greatest danger to be guarded against. And at the Colombo conference in January 1950, Nehru stated that "although Communism is bad, colonialism is infinitely worse."[6]

[5] *Economist,* June 24, 1950, Vol. CLVIII, p. 1392.
[6] *Economist,* June 3, 1950, Vol. CLVIII, p. 1225.

Will the United States be able to defeat the Russian efforts to foster Communism in all parts of the world and, in particular, to turn all non-Communist countries against us? Shall we be able to help non-Communist countries develop their industries and raise their standard of living? Shall we be able to do this without arousing the fear that we are attempting to undermine their independence? Can the United States help other countries develop their industries without weakening its own economy? In fact, can the United States make closer economic relations with other countries a source of strength to itself as well as to them?

How Can Other Countries Be Helped?

The task of preventing the spread of Communism is a stupendous one in a world where most people live in extreme poverty and have little immediate hope of anything better. Communism asserts that it will bring a vast improvement in the standard of living and paints a vivid picture of gains. Its attraction for many millions of persons undoubtedly is not its philosophy, which they do not know about or understand, but the fact that its champions show some concern for the condition of poverty-stricken people and offer a program for improving their condition. The people to whom Communism appeals for support are usually unable to judge the merits of its proposals. Indeed, they have had little or no experience in judging economic or political proposals. But many oppressed persons find that the champions of Communism are the first persons who have shown much interest in their condition and who have made proposals for improving it.

To combat the Utopias promised by the Communists there must be immediate and tangible improvement in living conditions and prospect of continued improvement. Consequently, the United States, as the principal opponent of Communism, needs to undertake the enormous task of stimulating and assisting economic progress in all non-Communist countries. Ever since the end of the Second World War this country has been giving aid on a huge scale. From the middle of 1945 until the end of 1949, the United States had given other countries grants or credits of no less than 25.9 billion dollars.[7] About three fifths of this amount took the form of grants and two fifths of credits. Some of the "credits" will undoubtedly turn out to be gifts. More than twenty billion dollars of the help was given to countries in Europe. Much of the aid has been given under the European Recovery Program, but even before the beginning of this program in 1948 the United States had been giving aid at the rate of more than five billion dollars a year.

The assistance that the United States has given other countries up to now has been stopgap in nature. It has been designed to meet the urgent needs for food, clothing, fuel, and capital goods caused by the disorganization of economic activities and the destruction of plant and equipment by the Second World War. This stopgap program must be re-

[7] "Report of the Advisory Council on International Monetary and Financial Problems, October 1, 1949–March 31, 1950," *Federal Reserve Bulletin*, August 1950, Vol. 36, p. 971.

placed by more permanent arrangements for helping other countries. A permanent program for raising the standard of living throughout the world cannot be based indefinitely upon gifts by the United States. The huge gifts that this country has been making are a heavy drain on our resources and a burden to American taxpayers. They have been roughly equal to the interest on the Federal debt. The gifts involve, however, a bigger burden than interest payments on the debt because they result in goods' leaving the country, whereas payment of interest on the debt involves only the transfer of goods within our economy.

The indefinite continuation of gifts would not be satisfactory to other countries. No country likes to depend indefinitely on gifts for part of its standard of living. Almost as undesirable as gifts are credits granted by the government. No one loves his creditors. Hence, aid in the form of government credits would not usually help the United States win or keep friends. In a few cases government loans may fit into a special program of assistance and might be granted upon the condition that the recommended program be carried out. Such conditional loans have been recommended by the economic survey mission to the Philippines, headed by Daniel W. Bell, former Undersecretary of the Treasury.[8]

[8] A not uncommon dilemma arises from the fact that the attachment of conditions to aid may arouse resentment at the interference of the United States in the affairs of other countries and that failure to attach conditions may cause the help to do more harm than good because the perpetuation of bad practices is encouraged. The following well-informed British opinion of the consequences of American aid to China is illuminating: "American aid to Nationalist China did not merely fail to put things right; it definitely made

As a general rule, however, help in the form of loans can probably be better given through the International Bank for Reconstruction and Development than through direct government credits. The Bank has made more than 700 million dollars of development loans. It has emphasized that none of these loans could have been privately financed. Nevertheless, none of these loans have encountered any servicing difficulties. The good record is attributable to the fact that the Bank insists on "well-prepared and well-planned projects ready for immediate execution," on the loan's being for a "sound and productive purpose," and on a prior appraisal of the capacity of the country to service the debt involved. Outright gifts are undoubtedly preferable to loose credits.

There is no one best way of helping other countries increase their output per capita and hence their standard of living. There are some countries where conditions for investment are excellent — where there is plenty of managerial skill, where the government is honest and efficient, and where there are good opportunities to make goods that can be readily sold in the United States; their great need is for capital goods and investment-seeking funds from abroad. Canada is an example, though part of the time in

---

them worse. By handing out large-scale economic assistance without conditions or supervision, the United States removed any pressure on the Kuomintang to put its house in order. Chinese leaders felt no need to carry out fiscal, administrative or political reforms; they relied on American funds to see them through their economic difficulty and to maintain their power in defiance of public opinion and criticism." (*Economist*, July 1, 1950, Vol. CLIX, p. 23.)

recent years Canada has been an exporter of capital. Where the conditions are generally favorable for investment and for making goods that can be sold in the United States, there is really no problem, because private capital from this country readily enters. There are other countries where the greatest economic need is merely better opportunities to sell to the United States. These countries have plenty of internal sources of capital and much managerial and technical skill, but they are limited in their ability to obtain some kinds of goods and to meet some of their obligations by their difficulties in earning dollars. Britain, Italy, and France are examples. In these instances the solution of the problem is in the reduction of obstacles to imports into this country.

The difficulties of raising output per capita are greatest where local capital is scarce, where knowledge of modern technology is meager, where there are few businessmen who have managerial skills and who are interested in gradually building up productive enterprises rather than in making a quick trading profit, where governments are corrupt and administration is bad, and where aroused nationalistic feeling makes the country unwilling to accept loans subject to foreign inspection or supervision of how the money is spent or the enterprise managed. Some or all of these handicaps to effective help from the United States or any other country exist in large parts of the world.

The United States must fit its procedures to the facts in each case. But the most effective single way in which we can stimulate production throughout the world, win much-needed friends for ourselves, and discourage the spread of Communism, is by increasing our imports. A large increase of sales to the United States would improve employment abroad and create opportunities for men to move into better jobs. It would enable other countries to earn dollars with which to buy equipment for their industries. It would strengthen the currencies of other countries and encourage the relaxing of exchange controls. It would furnish a foundation for direct investments by Americans in other countries and for private loans to other countries — since willingness to make investments or loans depends upon the possibility of transferring income from investments out of the country. It would make possible an early termination of outright grants from the United States and would replace the present relationship of donor-receiver with the more satisfactory and dignified relationship of buyer-seller. Certainly foreign countries are more likely to be friendly to us if this country is a large customer than if they are beholden to us for aid or owe our government large sums.

A rise of imports into the United States would reduce the cost to this country of fighting Communism. Part of this cost is represented by the goods that we send abroad for which we get no goods in return. In 1949, for example, this country exported about 6 billion dollars more goods and services than it imported. If a dollar of imports had been received for every dollar of exports, the volume of goods available for consumption here would have been 6 billion dollars greater, and the standard of living would have been that much higher. Many people, quite naturally, are quite concerned lest the huge cost of the fight against Communism drain our resources and lower our standard of living.

To the extent that the fight against Communism compels us to send abroad goods for which other goods are not received in return, it is a drain on our resources.

CAN IMPORTS INTO THE UNITED STATES BE SUBSTANTIALLY INCREASED?

But can imports into the United States be substantially increased? Undoubtedly imports will grow about as rapidly as the national product, which is normally about 3 per cent to 3.5 per cent a year and which may be around 4 per cent a year during the next decade. A "substantial" increase in imports, however, would be a faster growth than this. Can imports be raised at least moderately faster than the growth in the net national product? Many economists doubt it. Many kinds of imports, such as cheap iron ore, copper or lumber, would probably accelerate the increase of the national product here, thus limiting the tendency for imports to grow faster than the national product. No one, of course, would be sorry about that kind of rise in imports. Doubts about the possibility of increasing imports arise principally because of the conditions that hinder other countries from selling to us. The United States is a large country with a wide variety of resources and a wide range of climates. Its large population enables enterprises to use methods of production that would not pay in smaller markets. Finally, the high productivity of labor in this country tends, to a certain extent, to make labor even more productive. By giving tens of millions of persons fairly high incomes, it enables them to buy large quantities of goods that in other countries are luxury goods — automobiles, washing machines, electric refrigerators. Consequently, it permits these goods to be made by mass production methods. As a result of these conditions (rich and varied resources, a wide range of climates, mass production methods), imports into the United States, as I have pointed out, have been small in relation to the net national output and have been growing relatively smaller. Economists who doubt the possibility of substantially increasing our imports ask, "What kinds of imports might be increased and where would they come from?"

A persuasive case can be made for the view that a large increase of imports into this country can occur within a few years provided the American people are willing to let the goods come in and do not insist that the tariff be raised to keep them out. Of course, the surplus of exports over imports will persist, no matter how great the increase in imports, so long as this country gives aid to foreign countries, because the help given by the United States is simply a way of financing an export surplus. Consequently, as this country succeeds in increasing its imports, it should gradually reduce its grants to other countries.

What are the reasons for believing that the United States can substantially increase its imports? One reason is that the reciprocal trade agreements have brought about large reductions in American duties. It is true that many duties are still high, but large cuts have been made. The war and its aftermath, however, have delayed the effect of the tariff reductions upon the sales of other countries in the American market.

A second reason is the recent devaluation of many foreign currencies which has greatly improved the competitive position of foreign sellers in the American market. The immediate effect of devaluation is mainly to limit the ability of other countries to buy from us rather than to increase their ability to sell to us. But in the long run, the devaluation should greatly help other countries sell to this country.

A third reason is the rapidly growing consumption of raw materials by this country. The fact that the United States produces about half of the manufactured goods of the world and consumes about 40 per cent of the total output of the world means that it is bound to draw heavily upon other countries for raw materials. During the next thirty years the United States will consume as much raw material as in the past 150 years. Large increases in imports of oil, iron ore, bauxite, tin, copper, sugar, coffee, cocoa, and semimanufactured goods, such as lumber and wood pulp, are inevitable.

A fourth reason is the strong and aggressive trade union movement in the United States. The unions here are likely to raise wages and labor costs faster than the unions in most other countries — especially in those countries which are trying to raise their exports relative to their imports and which, in consequence, are placing restraints upon collective bargaining. In other words, although technological progress in the United States may be more rapid than in most other countries, labor costs here are likely to rise faster than in most countries.

The prospect for increasing imports into the United States would be improved if there were a repeal of the law

requiring the Federal government to buy only goods manufactured or mined in the United States or made of domestic materials. The prospect would also be improved if
the remaining high duties were substantially cut and if customs administration were simplified. The customs regulations are often as important an impediment to sales to the
United States as high duties, because the regulations often
prevent prospective sellers and buyers from knowing what
the actual duty would be.

How much of an increase in imports into this country
can be achieved? It is not unreasonable to assume that at
least 10 per cent of the commodities consumed here
could be produced more cheaply abroad, including in
foreign production costs the freight to this country. If only
one tenth of the commodities (as distinguished from services) consumed here came from abroad, merchandise imports would be running at the rate of over 14 billion dollars
a year instead of 7.5 billion, as in 1949, or about 8.0 billion,
as in 1950. Indeed, it would not be surprising to discover
that foreign countries could undersell domestic producers on
nearly 15 per cent of the commodities consumed in this
country. This does not mean that foreign sellers would
completely displace American producers in these fields
— it would mean that on certain grades or in certain parts
of the United States the sales of foreign-made goods would
be large. To the extent that foreign countries sold us more
goods, their purchases of American-made products would
rise.

A rapid increase of imports into the United States is not
likely. The recent cuts in duties and the currency devalua-

tions will produce their effects only over a period of years. Time will be required for foreign sellers to find out about American markets and for American manufacturers, distributors, and consumers to find out about buying opportunities abroad. Undoubtedly the best way to introduce many kinds of finished goods into the American market (particularly nonspecialty goods sold to individual consumers) is through the development of buying offices abroad by large American distributors. Many foreign manufacturers are likely to find that the cost of establishing branches or sales offices in this country is prohibitive. A chain store or group of department stores, however, can buy goods abroad and sell them in the United States at little or no greater marketing cost than the same goods purchased in New York. Furthermore, if goods are made to the specifications of American buyers, they are more likely to be acceptable to American consumers.

What Kind of Imports Will Increase?

The kind of goods that come into the United States has changed greatly in the course of time. In the early eighteen-eighties, for example, only about one third of our imports were raw materials and nearly two thirds were either semi-manufactured goods or finished manufactured goods. Finished manufactures (other than manufactured food products) made up about one third of all merchandise imports. Raw materials have been slowly becoming more important as imports, and finished manufactures less important. Shortly before the Second World War, nearly half of all imports were raw materials and less than one fifth of all imports were finished manufactured goods.

Technological progress in the United States and the growing capacity of the country to manufacture raw materials into finished goods will continue to increase our dependence upon foreign sources of raw materials. The United States, which uses about twice as much petroleum and as much steel and copper as all other countries combined, can hardly expect to draw entirely on its own supplies of oil, iron ore, or copper. In some cases, of course, the progress of technology will diminish our dependence upon foreign sources of raw materials or semimanufactured goods — as in the case of rubber and silk. Wool may soon have to be added to that list.

Among semimanufactured goods there are excellent opportunities for large increases in the imports of aluminum and lumber. Canada can produce aluminum at less cost than the United States. About one third of the aluminum consumed here might come from Canada. This would require roughly a quadrupling of Canadian aluminum sales to us. The United States is consuming far more lumber each year than the annual growth of its forests. A tenfold increase in imports would still leave about two thirds of the demand to be met by domestic output.

There are some possibilities of a considerable increase in food products. Cheese, lemons, wine, and cream are examples of food products excluded by high duties. Only about one tenth of the cheese consumed in the United States comes from abroad, but other countries make better cheese than we do and the American consumer should have the opportunity to buy foreign-made cheese without paying the equivalent of a stiff sales tax on it. At one time nearly all of the lemons used in the United States came from abroad but a high duty now severely limits imports. A large rise in the purchase of lemons from Italy would be in the national interest. Almost all of the wine consumed here is domestically produced, but, if the duty were cut, chain stores would be able to give American consumers good foreign wine at very moderate prices. As late as 1926 Canada had a moderately important cream export business to the United States. The tariff and customs procedure have virtually eliminated all Canadian cream from American markets.

In the main, however, the increase of imports into the United States will probably have to consist of finished manufactured goods. There are great possibilities of increases in these fields. Parts for automobiles might be made in southern Ontario as well as in Michigan or Indiana or Ohio. Many foreign-made textiles are superior to most American-made goods. If only one tenth of the worsteds consumed in this country came from abroad, imports of these products would increase about fivefold. If foreign countries supplied one tenth of the cotton cloth, imports would increase over ten times. Foreign countries should be able to make many articles of apparel — shirts, neckties, shoes, hose, underwear, hats — as cheaply as the United States. If these articles were made to American specifications for large buyers here, a considerable quantity of apparel could be imported. Foreign makers of china and pottery are able to produce at costs that are competitive with American costs, and only very stiff duties keep down imports to about one sixth of the domestic consumption. Cuts in duties sufficient to permit a doubling of imports would still leave the market largely in the hands of domestic producers.

WILL THE PEOPLE OF THE UNITED STATES TOLERATE A LARGE INCREASE IN IMPORTS?

Will the people of the United States tolerate a large rise in imports? A generation ago they certainly would not have done so. Today the answer to the question is in doubt. That in itself is an encouraging fact. The pressure to keep out foreign goods, no matter how large and plain the need for them, is enormous — as is plainly shown by the restoration of excise taxes on imported oil and copper in the summer of 1950 and the refusal of the National Security Resources Board in November 1950 to accept Canada as a source of increased aluminum supply. The Canadian government had proposed a contract under which Canada would guarantee to deliver aluminum to the United States at about 14 per cent below the prevailing price here on the following schedule: 35,000 tons in 1951, 65,000 tons in 1952, 100,000 tons in 1953, and thereafter any amount desired up to 500,000 tons a year. An ironic aspect of the decision of the National Security Resources Board is that it was made only about two weeks after the United States and Canada had signed an agreement binding both to pool their national resources in the struggle against Communism.

Of some help in keeping down duties may be the pleas

of our government that western Europe work out a plan of "integration." Indeed, in the European aid act of 1949 Congress declared that an aim of the law was to "encourage the integration of Europe." In October 1949, Paul G. Hoffman of the Economic Cooperation Administration, addressing the Marshall Plan Council in Paris, urged economic "integration" of Europe. Mr. Hoffman made it clear that "integration" meant removal of quantitative restrictions on imports fairly soon and the eventual removal of tariffs among the several European countries. He set no dates but he spoke repeatedly of the urgency of the issue.[9] The Europeans also have their ideas about integration. Some of them would like to integrate the United States, that is to include this country in an area free from trade barriers.

A large increase in imports would be good for the economy of the United States and would help raise the standard of living both here and abroad. It would enable other countries to specialize to a greater extent in turning out goods that they produce particularly well or cheaply — aluminum,

[9] In October 1949 the European countries agreed on cutting import quotas by 50 per cent by December 15, 1949. The quotas were cut by the required amount, but not by the agreed-on date. In January 1950, the European participants in the Marshall Plan undertook to remove another 10 per cent of the import quotas and to consider in July 1950 whether they would remove 75 per cent of the import quotas. Both of these decisions to liberate trade excluded the state-controlled imports that in Britain form about 27 per cent of all imports and in France about 21 per cent. The January decision on removing import quotas was made dependent on the creation of the payments union. (*New York Times,* March 5, 1950, Section 4, p. 5.)

wool, worsteds, cheese, wine, china, and many others — and to increase their purchases of machinery, automobiles, radio, and other articles from the United States, thus enabling this country to specialize somewhat more in producing the goods that it is best able to make. The increase in imports would also make competition brisker and this would stimulate technological progress in the United States. But one should not be too optimistic about the effects of larger imports into the United States upon the rest of the world. The more advanced countries would benefit enormously, but the help to backward countries would be limited. Undoubtedly the greatest ally of Communism is the high birth rate in many parts of the world. The United States can do little about this, but until the birth rate in India, China, and many other countries drops, output per capita will increase only slowly.

The various industries that would feel the competition of larger imports into the United States will strive vigorously to prevent the increase. They will demand higher duties and will also seek to use the administration of the tariff to keep out goods. For example, ingenious and far-fetched classifications of articles may be used, as at present, to impose higher duties on articles than would be imposed if they were classified by their normal uses.

The American people must make up their minds whether they wish to pursue international economic policies that re-enforce or those that undermine their international political policies. The United States has little choice except to do the best it can to halt the spread of Communism in a world where two thirds of the people live in dire poverty and see little hope of improvement in their condition. The task of raising productivity and standards of living throughout the world is a stupendous one. The United States cannot be expected to drain its resources indefinitely by gifts to the rest of the world — and gifts, as I have indicated, may not be very effective in winning friends. The most practical way for the United States to help the rest of the world, and at the same time to help itself, is to buy goods in huge quantities. Perhaps the increasingly intense conflict with Russia will lead the people of this country to take a broad and realistic view of foreign policy, to disregard the outcries of the special interests that would undermine the country's foreign policy in order to win protection from foreign competition, and to insist that our international political policies be backed up with appropriate economic policies.

CHAPTER VI

The Capacity of Our Economy to Grow

In the last fifty years the economy of the United States has expanded rapidly. Output per man-hour has considerably more than trebled and the labor force and the volume of employment, as I pointed out in Chapter III, have grown a little faster than the population of working age — that is, the population of 14 years of age or more.

Yet in spite of rapid growth of production and employment, many people have grave doubts about the capacity of the economy to expand rapidly enough. These doubts take two very different forms. Many are afraid that the number of jobs will not grow fast enough to provide work for the increasing number of job seekers. Others fear that the output of industry will fail to expand rapidly enough to meet the ever-growing need for goods, especially goods for defense, and that the standard of living of the people will suffer.

The doubts concerning the ability of the economy to increase jobs as rapidly as the number of job seekers grows are shared by persons of sharply differing economic philosophies. Many radicals, for example, believe that the capacity of the economy to grow is limited by an excessive disposition to save that limits the demand for consumer goods and thus in turn limits the demand for capital goods. Many conservatives, on the other hand, believe that the expansion of the economy is retarded by high taxes and bad public policies which weaken the incentive to increase production — particularly as to starting new enterprises — and which discourage the accumulation of investment-seeking funds. Doubts about the capacity of the economy to meet the ever-growing demand for goods have been strengthened by the worsening relations between the United States and Russia and the necessity for greatly increased expenditures on defense and foreign military aid. Many people fear that such a large part of national output will be required for defense that the expansion of industrial plant and equipment will be substantially retarded and thus the rise in the country's standard of living will be held back.

How rapidly does the economy need to grow? What are the principal conditions which now limit or are likely to limit its growth? How can the obstacles to growth be removed or, at least, reduced in importance?

It is convenient to break up the general question of how fast the economy needs to grow into three principal parts: (1) How rapidly should the number of jobs increase in order to provide employment for all who wish to work? (2) How rapidly does output per man-hour need to grow in order to enable the standard of living of the country to rise at a satisfactory rate? and (3) How rapidly does the money demand for goods need to expand in order to enable the country to make full use of its growing productive capacity?

How Much of an Increase in the Number of Jobs?

One is tempted to assert that the number of jobs needs to grow as fast as the labor force. But this is not satisfactory because the number of people who would like to work may be considerably larger than the number who are in the labor force. The reason is that the size of the labor force is determined in part by the number of jobs available. Hence if the number of jobs were to grow more rapidly, the labor force would grow more rapidly — at least up to a certain point. The strength of the demand for labor has a particularly strong influence upon the number of older persons who are at work. When the demand for labor is strong, many persons who would have been retired by their employers and who would have left the labor force on retirement, even though preferring to work, are kept on beyond the age of retirement. This happened in many plants during the Second World War. Likewise, many persons who are retired by their employers will seek and obtain other work. Indeed, the movement in and out of the labor force among older persons is considerably larger than is generally realized. During the first seven months of 1950, for example, there were 1,536,000 entrances into the labor force among persons of 65 years of age or over.[1] Furthermore, if the

[1] In the same period there were 1,583,000 withdrawals from the labor force among persons of 65 years of age or more.

number of jobs available in the vicinity increases, many persons who have not been in the labor force, particularly women, will accept jobs. This happens when a new plant starts up in a community. It also happens when existing plants increase the number of their jobs.

How many people who are not members of the labor force would gladly work if jobs, paying the going rate, were available? I venture the guess that there are at least 2.5 million such persons. This rough estimate or guess is based upon the conclusion that the number of women of all working ages and the number of males of 65 years of age or over in the labor force are considerably less than would gladly work. The number of women who would work, if jobs similar to existing ones were available, is at least as high a proportion of women of working age as were employed during the war. It is conservative to estimate that three out of five males of 65 years of age or more would rather work than retire. The fact that industry has not attracted into the labor force the persons who would like to work costs the country an enormous loss of production — probably as much as 8 billion dollars a year. This is far more than the loss from all the featherbed rules of all the unions in the country.

The proportion of women of working age (14 years or over) in the labor force in 1950 was 33.2 per cent; in 1944, in the midst of the war, it was 36.8 per cent. The proportion varies from month to month — the above figures are the average for the year. I have suggested that the proportion of women who would willingly accept work is at least as high as the wartime percentage. It is true that the propor-

tion of the younger women at work might not reach wartime levels, but there are great possibilities of increasing the
number of jobholders among women of 45 years of age and
over. In July 1950, for example, only 32.3 per cent of
the women of 45 to 64 years of age were in the labor
force.[2] In 1930, the proportion was less than 20 per cent;
by 1944, it was 31.6 per cent and the proportion did not
drop when the demand for labor decreased after the war —
in fact, the proportion increased. It seems plain that working is gaining considerably in popularity among older
women.

My estimate that the proportion of males of 65 years of
age or more in the labor force can be increased to about
60 per cent is based upon the fact that back in 1890 the
proportion stood as high as 68.2 per cent, and upon the
additional fact that the subsequent drop in the proportion
of older men in the labor force has occurred, not at the
volition of the employees, but at the decision of employers.[3]
Men who are in good health usually prefer employment at
their customary jobs to retirement even on liberal pensions.

[2] Among girls of 14 to 19 years of age the proportion in the
labor force increased from 23.3 per cent in 1940 to 41.8 per cent in
1944, and dropped to 32.5 per cent in 1949. Among women of 20 to
24 years of age, the proportion in the labor force increased from
49.5 per cent in 1940 to 54.0 per cent in 1944, and dropped to 45.0
per cent in 1949.

[3] The estimate that 68.2 per cent of males of 65 years of age or
over were in the labor force in 1890 is that of John D. Durand in
The Labor Force in the United States, 1890–1960, p. 208. It is
smaller than the census figures because Mr. Durand adjusted the
census figures to make them comparable with 1940 census data.

A recent survey by one of the staff of the Social Security Agency showed that among a group of men receiving Federal old-age pensions, only about one out of twenty had retired of his own volition when he was in good health. About one out of three retired because of poor or failing health, but more than half said that they were retired by their employers.[4] Although the proportion of men of 65 years of age or more in the labor force dropped to 42.2 per cent in April 1940, it rose to nearly 50 per cent in response to the strong wartime demand for labor. By 1950 the proportion was back to about 45 per cent. If it were raised to 60 per cent, the labor force would be increased by about 750,000 men.

If the proportion of women in the labor force were raised to 36 per cent (not quite the ratio of 1944) and the proportion of males of 65 years of age or over in the labor force to 60 per cent, the total labor force by 1960 would be nearly 75 million — an increase of over 10 million above the labor force in 1950.[5] This is a good measure of the increase

[4] E. C. Wentworth, "Why Beneficiaries Retire," *Social Security Bulletin,* January 1945, p. 16. The low proportion of voluntary retirements might have been influenced by the fact that only small pensions were then available under the Federal Old Age and Survivors' Insurance Plan, but this was probably not the case. Even where pensions are liberal, the proportion of voluntary retirements is low.

[5] The estimate of the labor force is the monthly average for the year. The estimates of population in 1960 are the recently revised estimates of the Bureau of the Census. They assume medium fertility and mortality, 350,000 net annual immigration for 1949–1950, and 200,000 thereafter. U.S. Bureau of the Census, *Current Population Report,* Series P–25, No. 43, p. 6.

in the number of jobs that will be needed by 1960. My estimate of the increase in the labor force between 1950 and 1960 is somewhat larger than other estimates. For example, Mr. John D. Durand has estimated that the labor force would increase about 4,760,000 between 1950 and 1960.[6] In the decade 1960 to 1970, when the labor force will feel the influence of the births between 1940 and 1950, the increase in the number of workers will again be large — about 9 million.

An obstacle to raising the proportion of older persons at work is the fact that their productivity is usually less than that of younger workers. If a man's productivity at age 68 is one fourth or one third less than it was at the age of 50, the employer can scarcely afford to pay him standard wages. And yet for the country as a whole it is far better that he produce two thirds or three fourths of a day's work than be retired on a pension producing nothing at all. The decline in the productivity of older workers may not cause serious trouble in plants where men are paid by the piece; but where payment is by the hour, the employer may be compelled to retire older workers in order to avoid paying them more than they are worth. A way is needed to pro-

[6] John D. Durand, *The Labor Force in the United States, 1890–1960*, p. 257. As Mr. Durand estimated a population of 121,840,000 persons of 14 years of age or over in 1960, he was estimating that about 53.4 per cent of the population of working age would be in the labor force. Mr. Durand's estimates are derived by using pre-war trends that do not reflect the effect of the war upon the desire of people to work. He expresses the view (pp. 19–20) that the influences that led to an abnormal increase in the labor force during the war will be temporary.

tect the community from losing the output of older workers and to enable the men themselves to continue to work
as long as they prefer working to retirement.

There are several ways of reducing the number of premature retirements. One way would be for unions to bargain for pension plans with a higher age of retirement.
This is now being done by a few unions. The United Automobile Workers have negotiated pension agreements with
the General Motors Corporation and the Ford Motor Company that provide for two ages of retirement. The worker
may draw a pension on retiring at the age of 65 (provided
he has been in the employ of the company for a given
number of years), but the company does not have the right
to retire him until he has reached the age of 68.[7] The Oscar
Mayer Packing Company has negotiated an agreement in
which the usual age of retirement is 70.

Another way of reducing the number of premature retirements is to encourage the spread of piece work. Under
this method of payment, a man's earnings drop automat-
ically as his output decreases. Hence the direct labor cost
to the employer is the same for a slow worker as for a fast
one. Of course, the overhead per unit of output is greater
in the case of slow employees, but the disadvantage to the
employer in having some slow workers is much less than
when payment is by the hour.

Still another way of reducing premature retirements is to
give the employer a subsidy for each worker he retains
beyond a given age. This would compensate the em-

[7] The company may, of course, drop the man at any age because
of inefficiency.

ployer for the fact that many men, who are able to do useful work, are not able to produce enough to be worth their wages. It has been suggested that the subsidy take the form of a rebate in the corporate income tax if a given portion of the working force were more than a specified age, say 65. A better arrangement would probably be a payment to the employer for each worker retained beyond a given age, say 68. It might be one fifth or one fourth of the earnings of the worker. A subsidy of this amount would give the employer a strong incentive to keep men who were quite productive though no longer worth their wages. The retention of workers who might otherwise be pensioned would save money for the Federal old-age and survivors' pension scheme, since men who were employed would not be drawing pensions. Hence, the cost of the subsidies should be paid by the old-age and survivors' pension plan. The total money costs of pensions and subsidies under this plan would probably be about the same as the cost of pensions alone under a plan that gave the employer no incentive not to retire workers.[8] The community as a whole

[8] Studies of the Federal Security Agency show that at the beginning of 1950 about 55 per cent of all men aged 65 to 69 inclusive who were eligible for old-age and survivors' insurance benefits had not claimed them; of those 74 to 75 years of age, 32 per cent had not claimed benefits; and of those 75 years of age or more, 18 per cent had not claimed benefits. The average age of the men who were retiring and first claiming old-age insurance benefits was 68.5 years, These figures indicate that it will probably not be necessary to subsidize the employment of workers below the age of 68.

A few employees will not be eligible for pensions under the old-age and survivors' insurance plan. In such cases the subsidy paid to

would be ahead by the amount of the production of the men
who otherwise would have been retired.

THE NEED FOR MORE OUTPUT PER MAN-HOUR

The need for more output per man-hour is virtually
unlimited because there seems to be scarcely any limit to
the capacity of men to consume goods. The average family,
among the fifth of the families with the largest incomes,
spent in 1949 about 6700 dollars on consumer goods. If the
lowest four fifths of the families had consumed the same
quantity of goods per family as was consumed by the
highest fifth, the output of consumer goods would have
had to be doubled. And yet the families that spend about
6700 dollars a year have no difficulty in finding ways to
spend their money. It is plain that the output of American
industry might be much more than doubled without satis-
fying the need for goods.

The rate at which output per man-hour increases depends
upon (1) the personal efficiency with which men do their
work (care, application); (2) the plant rules governing the
use of labor; (3) the progress of technological research;
(4) the rate at which old equipment is replaced with new
and better equipment; and (5) the rate at which capital
per worker is increased.

If the country succeeds in maintaining a strong sellers'

---

the employer for the retention of the worker beyond the age of
68 should be a charge against the old-age assistance appropriation,
not the old-age and survivors' scheme.

market most of the time, the personal efficiency of workers is likely to drop unless managements take special steps to prevent it. Unfortunately many managements are reluctant to insist on high standards of performance at a time when labor is scarce. Their reluctance has been enhanced by their difficulty in getting labor arbitrators to back up managements in disputes arising out of discipline for bad work. Perhaps managements will gradually learn that it is short-sighted to tolerate low standards of workmanship and responsibility, and labor arbitrators will gradually learn that the standard of living of the country suffers when managements are not able to enforce high standards of responsibility and efficiency. The general rule should be that a man is entitled to one warning, but thereafter deviations from a high standard of care and application should be subject to discipline.

The plant rules governing the use of labor in American industry are generally free from make-work arrangements. Nevertheless, a few powerful unions, such as some of the railroad unions, the longshoremen, and the musicians, have been quite aggressive in seeking to enforce make-work rules. Some economists believe that a continuation of a high level of employment will weaken the interest of unions in make-work rules. I believe that the effect of high employment will be the opposite — that the strong bargaining position of unions will encourage them to demand and obtain more and more make-work rules. The reason is that many of the proposed make-work rules do not arise out of fear of unemployment — they are designed to accelerate promotions. In periods of strong demand for goods, managements are tempted to yield to the demand for wasteful rules and to pass on the costs in the form of higher prices. If make-work rules threaten to become widespread, the government may need to declare them contrary to public policy and to establish machinery to prohibit them.

Far more important than the personal efficiency of labor or the rules governing the use of labor are the rate of technological progress, the rate at which old equipment is replaced with new, and the increase in capital per worker. Technological research, as I have indicated in Chapter III, has been growing rapidly and will continue to grow rapidly, partly because research by one concern forces its rivals to engage in research and partly because the strong upward pressure of unions on wages stimulates enterprises to look for methods of increasing productivity.

The rate at which old plant and equipment are replaced with new is likely to be more rapid in the future than in the past. High tax rates on corporate income make it advantageous for enterprises to scrap old equipment at an earlier age. Indeed, rising labor costs and high corporate income taxes are likely to cause many companies to review their replacement policies, which, as W. J. Kelly of the Machinery and Allied Products Institute has well said, are "the product of intellectual folklore handed down from one generation to another."

The rate at which capital per worker is increased is likely to be no less rapid than it has been. Giving men more capital (that is, more plant, equipment, and inventories) to help them produce is an obvious way of increasing their output. Included in plant are housing, roads, and various public works, as well as industrial plant in the narrow sense. But will the country be able to provide sufficient investment-seeking funds to finance the growth in capital per worker? It is difficult to determine what is a normal rate of growth because the actual rate seems to have varied considerably from decade to decade. In the twenties, when the rate of increase was not retarded by wars or business depression, plant, equipment, and inventories per worker (in 1950 dollars) increased from less than 9800 dollars in 1920 to about 10,700 in 1929, or 10.2 per cent. It ought to be possible to maintain as rapid a rate of increase in capital per worke.· as occurred in the twenties. The same annual rate of increase, between 1950 and 1960, combined with a rise of over 10 million in the labor force during the same period, would mean a growth of about 190 billion (in 1950 dollars) in plant, equipment, and inventories.[9] This growth would absorb about 6.0 per cent of the net national product. This is considerably less than the proportion of the net national product devoted to increasing capital between 1920 and

[9] Total capital in July 1950 was about 10,188 dollars per member of the labor force, or 658.2 billion dollars for the entire country. An increase between 1950 and 1960 at the same annual rate as between 1920 and 1929 would raise capital per worker to 11,343 dollars per member of the labor force, or 847.3 billion dollars in terms of July 1950 dollars. If output per man-hour increased at 2.5 per cent per year, and the average hours of work per week dropped to 41.0 in 1960, and if unemployment in 1960 averaged 5 per cent of the labor force, the net national product in 1960 would be 371.5 billion dollars in comparison with slightly less than 260 billion in 1950. The total net national product during the 10-year period would be approximately 3160 billion dollars.

1929, when the proportion was about 11.5 per cent. It looks as if the country would be well able to increase substantially plant, equipment, and inventories per worker.

Persons who fear that the increase in production will be held back by lack of investment-seeking funds point out that the ability of many persons to save is limited by the income tax, which now takes a considerable part of many incomes, but which was very low in the twenties. Most of the saving has always been done by persons in the higher income brackets, and among these persons the income tax has greatly reduced the ability to save. I have pointed out that the total income after taxes of persons receiving incomes of 25,000 dollars a year or more was one sixth less in 1948 than in 1928 — although the number of persons receiving incomes of 25,000 dollars a year or more was 60 per cent greater than in 1928. Even high income taxes, however, do not seem to have reduced the ability to save among the population as a whole. Indeed, in 1948 the ratio of personal savings to personal incomes even *before* taxes was higher than in 1929, and in 1949 it was about the same as in 1929. In 1929 personal savings were 4.3 per cent of personal incomes; in 1948, 5.2 per cent; and in 1949, 4.1 per cent.

The maintenance of the old rate of saving, despite high income taxes, is attributable to more saving among the middle and lower income groups. The increase in saving among these groups was probably a result of their desire to buy houses, which they were purchasing in large numbers, particularly in the years 1948, 1949, and 1950. In other words, if there are things that people strongly desire and that can be obtained only by saving, people will save. If the expansion of the plant and equipment of industry is ever held back by lack of thrift among individuals, one remedy for the problem would be for corporations to foster among millions of individuals the desire to own good securities. As a matter of fact, the problem is not likely to be acute, because a low rate of personal thrift would mean a strong demand for consumer goods, high corporate profits, and a high rate of corporate saving.

But is not this optimistic conclusion about the capacity of the country to increase plant, equipment, and inventories per worker as rapidly in the future as in the past made obsolete, for the next two or three years at least, by the quickened conflict between the United States and Russia that began with the Korean war? Will not the stiff increases in taxes on individuals and corporations made necessary by the huge military expenditures prevent industry from obtaining the funds needed for a rapid expansion of plant and equipment?

Of course mistakes in public policy may make it impossible for industry to finance large increases in productive capacity. If this happens, it will be tragic. The contest between the United States and Russia is a long-run production contest and it is important that we keep on rapidly increasing our productive capacity. As I have pointed out in Chapter II, however, expenditures on plant and equipment are not likely to be limited by lack of investment-seeking funds — though increases in taxes above the rates prevailing before the Korean war will be large and some of these increases will limit the ability of corporations to plow back earnings. The volume of expenditures on new plant and equipment will be determined fundamentally by the availability of materials and labor. Even these will probably be sufficient to permit the renewal and expansion of plant and equipment to continue at the high rate that prevailed during the second quarter of 1950.

The money to finance large outlays on plant and equipment will come from several sources. To some extent, even in the face of price ceilings, increases in the corporate income tax will be passed on. Enterprises engaged in essential defense production can obtain funds for reinvestment through accelerated depreciation allowances. Many corporations, as I have pointed out in Chapter II, can finance outlays on plant and equipment by the sale of government securities. At the end of September 1950, nonfinancial corporations held 19.4 billion dollars' worth of government securities. In some cases funds to reinvest in the business can be obtained by paying dividends in stock rather than cash. Some funds can be obtained by outside borrowing. The large number of pension funds that have been established in recent years will have income to invest. Furthermore, as I have explained in Chapter II, personal savings will grow — partly as a result of shortages of consumer goods and partly as a result of the repayment of the large volume of personal indebtedness that grew up between 1945 and 1950. Shortages of building materials and labor will reduce the proportion of personal savings spent on housing and thus increase the proportion devoted to industry. Finally, corporations will obtain investment funds, if necessary, by borrowing from commercial banks.

What about the fears that the expansion of the economy

will be retarded by too much saving? These fears were widespread during the depression of the thirties, which caused many people to believe that the expansion of the economy would be held back by excessive thriftiness — that the tendency for savings to outrun investment opportunities would keep employment and incomes low and thus keep the *absolute* amount of saving and investment low. Keynes has expressed this view in one of his most famous passages, which reads in part as follows: ". . . in contemporary conditions the growth of wealth, so far from being dependent on the abstinence of the rich, as is commonly supposed, is more likely to be impeded by it." [10]

The worsened relations between the United States and Russia make the fears of too much saving, generated by the great depression of the thirties, seem quite remote. This does not mean that bad international relations are necessary in order to make the economic institutions of America work — though one must admit that an end to the contest between the United States and Russia would cause some drop in the urgency of demand and some decline in the size of the labor force and in the volume of employment. One cannot expect, however, either the labor force or the number of jobs to be as large in a time of peace as in a time of emergency.

And yet the restoration of peace would not cause saving to become so large relative to investment opportunities as to prevent the maintenance of a reasonably satisfactory level of employment and a reasonably rapid growth in capital per

[10] *The General Theory of Employment, Interest and Money,* p. 373.

worker. There are several reasons for this conclusion. One is that less than half of all personal saving creates an investment problem — a fact that Keynes and his followers have overlooked. Most personal saving is for the purpose of buying some tangible capital asset — a house, or equipment for a farm or for some other business owned by the saver. Such saving does not create the need for investment opportunities because it is the result of a decision to invest. If the saver had not decided to buy the investment goods, he would undoubtedly have bought more consumer goods. In the years 1948 and 1949, the kind of personal savings that create an investment problem (savings seeking investment in corporate or government securities or going into insurance reserves, or savings and loan shares) amounted to a little more than 9 billion dollars. But expenditures of individuals on tangible capital assets were much larger — in 1948 individuals spent on nonfarm residences and on plant and equipment for unincorporated enterprises about 17.3 billion dollars and in 1949, about 16.3 billion. A second reason why an excessive disposition to save is not likely to limit the accumulation of capital is that nearly half of the investment-seeking funds are provided out of reinvested corporate profits. A drop in the volume of investment opportunities would cause corporations to use less of their profits for expansion and to pay out a larger fraction of their earnings in dividends. Hence a drop in investment opportunities would produce a quick drop in corporate savings.[11]

[11] The drop in corporate saving, however, may lag behind the drop in investment opportunities and cause, temporarily at least, some contraction in production. The lag might occur because cor-

One of the fears generated by the depression of the thirties was that, as the economy became wealthier and wealthier, it would find expansion more and more difficult to achieve. It was thought that, as incomes increased, the disposition to save would become more pronounced and would make the attainment of a high level of employment more and more difficult. These fears, however, are ill-founded. As the economy becomes wealthier, men have better opportunities for education. Although education encourages people to be foresighted, it is probably on balance bad for thrift. It gives people ideas on how to spend money; it makes them desire to live rich and full lives, to travel, to see the best that the world has to offer, to own beautiful and expensive things. All of these desires are bad for thrift. It is among primitive peoples that one finds the demand for goods so limited and so conventional that large earnings quickly cause the workers to spend less time at work.

Will Spending Keep Pace with Output?

Can the money demand for goods be increased fast enough to provide a market for the growing output of the expanding labor force and the improving technology? It is of little use to enlarge the labor force, to improve technology, and to increase capital per worker unless there is effective demand to absorb the increased output. I have suggested that the labor force might increase during the

porations were led by a drop in investment opportunities to use part of their retained profits to reduce their debts.

next ten years by about 10 million, or about 1.5 per cent a year, and output per man-hour by possibly 2.5 per cent a year. Should the length of the work week decline slowly and should the price level remain unchanged, the net national product would be almost 372 billion dollars in 1960. This would require an annual increase in the money demand for goods of about 4.0 per cent a year in order to absorb the increase in output. But if the rise in output were less, a smaller increase in the money demand for goods would suffice. On the other hand, if unions were to push up wages faster than output per man-hour rises, so that prices increased, a faster growth in the money demand for goods would be needed. For example, if the price level advanced by 2 per cent while the labor force increased by 1.5 per cent a year, output per man-hour by 2.5 per cent, and the work week declined slowly, the money demand for goods would need to grow by about 6 per cent a year.

The huge expenditures that the United States will be making on defense and foreign aid during the next several years will eliminate for the time being the problem of getting expenditures to keep pace with production. During this time the problem will be one of preventing expenditures from outrunning production. After two or three years, when defense expenditures take a decided drop, the problem of how to assure that spending grows as rapidly as the potential output of industry will again become of practical importance. Consequently, it is desirable to examine this problem.

Expenditures cannot grow unless some people are willing to spend at least a little bit more than their recent income — while other persons continue to spend the same amounts out of their incomes. The truth of this statement can be readily seen if one considers the relationship between incomes and expenditures. The incomes of today are simply the other side of the expenditures of today — when A buys from B, C, and D, he contributes to the incomes of B, C, and D. But if today's incomes are equal to today's expenditures, tomorrow's expenditures can rise above today's expenditures only if people are willing to spend tomorrow more than they received today in income. The core of the problem of getting adequate expansion of the economy, therefore, is to get some persons or organizations to spend a little bit more than their recent incomes. Many people, of course, spend *less* than their recent incomes on goods. Consequently, if the money demand for goods is to rise, the failure of some people or business concerns to spend all of their recent incomes must be more than offset by the willingness of other persons and enterprises to spend more than their incomes.

How can the community as a whole spend more than its recent income? There are three principal ways. One is by drawing on idle or inactive bank balances. A second is by selling securities to commercial banks which create the dollars to pay for them, or to individuals who pay for them out of inactive balances. Merely selling securities to individuals who purchase them out of current income does not increase the total expenditures for goods. The seller of the security has more to spend for goods but the buyer has less to spend. But when a commercial bank buys the security, the seller has more to spend and no one else has less to spend. A third way by which the community may spend more than its recent income is by borrowing from commercial banks. Obviously if A borrows from another individual, B, who lends part of his savings, there is no increase in spending because B has less to spend by the same amount that A has more to spend. But if A borrows from a commercial bank, A's increased supply of dollars is not offset by anyone else's saving.

Why should individuals or enterprises be willing to spend more than their recent incomes? It is sometimes assumed that expenditures on consumer goods are pretty completely determined by the size of personal incomes after taxes, and that the dynamic element in the economy (the spending of more than recent incomes) must be provided by business enterprises and the government. Keynes, for example, treats the demand for consumer goods as almost completely determined by the size of personal incomes and little affected by other conditions, such as expectations of changes in income or changes in the value of one's property. It is true that the kind of spending that is not closely determined by recent income is mainly done by business concerns rather than individuals. Nevertheless, even individual spending is not tied as closely to personal incomes as Keynes assumes. Frequently, individual expenditures in excess of recent income are the result of necessity — sickness or, in the case of retired persons, the necessity of living off one's capital. Or it may arise because of the desire to purchase expensive goods, such as houses, automobiles, or other consumer durable goods, which cannot be paid for entirely out of income. In both 1948 and 1949 slightly more than 3 out of every 10 spending units spent more than they earned, and the volume of personal indebtedness, though lower in relation to personal income than in 1929, was quite large. In 1949 over half of all spending units had debts of some kind — one out of five had mortgages on homes and more than one out of five had installment debt.

Most spending beyond recent incomes, however, is done by the government or by business enterprises. The expenditures of the Federal government and of most local and state governments have, of course, been rising with few interruptions since 1933. Business enterprises sometimes spend more than their incomes in order to build up inventories in advance of expected rises in prices. Their principal reason for spending more than their incomes, however, is to add to the capacity of their plants or to provide themselves with better equipment. Consequently, increases in expenditures by business concerns are closely related to technological discoveries that give enterprises opportunities to substitute new equipment for old or bring out new and improved products.

What are the prospects that the community, after the peak of defense expenditures has been reached and when military spending is dropping, will be willing to spend more than its recent income? I believe that they are good — in fact, that spending will probably grow more rapidly than physical production. There are five principal reasons for this conclusion.

1. *Personal holdings of cash and demand deposits are large in relation to expenditures for consumer goods.* Be-

tween the end of 1939 and the end of 1949, personal holdings of cash and demand deposits increased more than fourfold, from 11.4 billion to 47.6 billion dollars, but expenditures on consumer goods did not even treble. In 1939 they were 67.5 billion dollars; in 1949, 178.8 billion. If individuals were to spend cash and demand deposits for consumer goods as fast today as they did in 1939, the demand for consumer goods would rise enormously — from the annual rate of about 199 billion dollars in the middle of 1950 to 282 billion dollars a year. Such a rise would be disastrous if it occurred within a short period of time and it would be particularly disastrous if it occurred now. But the possibility that individuals can eventually be persuaded to spend part of their accumulations of cash on consumer goods indicates that for some years conditions will be favorable for an expansion of the demand for goods.

Many individuals will be reluctant to spend more than their recent incomes to buy consumer goods, but they might be willing to spend part of these accumulations for houses. Such expenditures would, of course, be quite as effective in increasing the total demand for goods as spending on consumer goods. Furthermore, many holders of cash and demand deposits may be persuaded to convert part of them into new corporate securities. This would make it unnecessary to finance all of the expansion of business plant and equipment out of current personal savings and would increase the money demand for goods accompanying a given expansion of investment.

2. *Holdings of government securities by individuals and business enterprises, other than banks, are very large.* In

September, 1950, more than 128.5 billion dollars of the debt of the Federal government was owned by individuals and non-bank corporations and associations. Back in 1940 non-bank corporations owned less than one fourth the quantity of government securities that they now own and individuals owned little more than one seventh.

These huge holdings of government securities are potential demand for goods because they can be sold to commercial banks or to the Federal Reserve Banks to pay for goods. Non-bank corporations have been gradually selling their government securities. Their holdings dropped from 66.4 billion dollars at the end of 1945 to 60.3 billion dollars in June 1950. Until recently individuals, however, have been purchasing government securities a little faster than they have been selling or redeeming them. Their holdings in July 1950 were larger than at the end of the war. Non-bank corporations will probably continue slowly to convert their holdings of government securities into goods. The more rapidly technological progress opens up new investment opportunities, the greater will be the rate at which non-bank corporations sell their government securities in order to buy new and better plants and equipment. Individuals, too, may reduce their holdings of government securities after the defense spending of the government drops — after about 1954. In that year the maturities of E bonds will probably be well in excess of 6 billion dollars (depending upon redemptions during the next several years) and in 1955, well in excess of 5 billion. In each of the following five years the maturities will probably be in excess of 2 billion dollars. The disposition of individuals to convert maturing bonds into goods will depend partly upon the success of industry in bringing out new and attractive products.

3. *The debts of individuals and corporations are low in relation to their incomes.* Consequently, both individuals and corporations will be willing to incur additional debts in order to increase their spending. In 1949 individuals had 50.0 cents of debt for each dollar of income after taxes in comparison with 88.0 cents in 1929 and 71.3 cents in 1940. Corporations, in 1949, had 31.0 cents of debt (both long-term and short-term) for each dollar of corporate sales in comparison with 64.1 cents in 1929 and 56.0 cents in 1940.

4. *The expenditures of the states and municipalities will continue to increase and part of this increase will be financed by borrowing.* The states and municipalities have always done much of their construction with borrowed money. When the defense expenditures of the Federal government drop, the high yield of taxes may produce a surplus for a year or two. For the reasons that I have pointed out in Chapter III, however, the Federal government will soon spend more than its cash receipts.

5. *The rate of technological improvement will be rapid, encouraging spending by business enterprises on new plant and equipment and by consumers on new goods, especially durable goods.* The reasons why technological change will be rapid were discussed in Chapter III.

How Rapidly will the Money Supply Need to Increase?

How much money will the commercial banks have to create in order to finance a rise in spending of about 4 per cent a year? The answer depends, in the main, upon how rapidly money changes hands. For many years the rate at which money changed hands was declining. If one assumes that the rate does not change, then an increase in expenditures of 4 per cent per year will require an increase in the money supply of 4 per cent a year. Since the money supply is about 180 billion dollars, the needed increase would be about 7.2 billion dollars a year for the next several years. Later the increase would need to be a little larger. If the rate at which money turns over were to continue to drop, the needed increase in the money supply would be greater. On the other hand, if the rate at which money is spent were to rise (as it may well do as a result of the expectation that prices will rise), the needed increase would be less — in fact, no increase might be needed at all.

If the net national product in 1960 is about 372 billion dollars and the rate at which money is spent does not change, the money supply would need to increase from about 180 billion, as in 1950, to about 260 billion in 1960 — a rise of 80 billion dollars. This would be much slower than the usual expansion in the money supply. If the rate at which money turns over were to drop, a larger increase in the money supply would be needed; if the rate of spending were to rise, the expansion would not need to be so large. If wage advances bring about a rise in labor costs, requiring an increase in the price level, the money supply will probably need to grow by considerably more than 80 billion. Some of the additions to the money supply would come from domestic gold production or from gold imports, but most of the new money would have to be created by the commercial banks.

The conclusion yielded by this examination of the capacity of the economy to grow is that the prospects of rapid growth are excellent. A moderate increase in the proportion of persons of working age who are in the labor force seems quite possible. The prospects are good that the output per man-hour will continue to grow as rapidly as in the recent past. Finally, the abnormally large personal holdings of cash and demand deposits in relation to expenditures for consumer goods, the large holdings of government securities by individuals and non-bank corporations, the abnormally small debts of individuals and corporations in relation to their income, and the prospect that the state, local, and Federal governments will more or less regularly spend a little bit more than they collect in taxes all indicate that the effective demand for goods should grow at least as rapidly as the capacity of the economy to produce goods.

CHAPTER VII

The Future Organization
of the Economy

WHAT WILL THE FUTURE ORGANIZATION of our economy and the distribution of power in it be like? Economic institutions and economic philosophies have been changing rapidly, and there are no signs that the rate of change is dropping. Where are we headed? Will the ultimate result be a socialist state, a planned economy, a welfare state, or some still other kind of economic organization?

There is no reason to expect that economic and political institutions will ever cease evolving. Hence one should not envisage any ultimate and permanent economic system, as did the nineteenth century Socialists or as do the Communists today. The countries which go far in adopting socialism can hardly be expected to keep it indefinitely, and even the police states will not be able to halt completely the development of social institutions or to control completely the course of evolution — for example, to prevent civil rights from eventually being established. Since the change in social institutions goes on indefinitely, let us explore the probable next steps in the development of the organization and control of our economy.

THE CHANCES OF SOCIALISM

Socialism of the kind envisaged by the nineteenth century Socialists, that is, government ownership and operation of most industries, does not seem likely to develop in the United States. To be sure, government ownership and operation of industries is likely to be important in countries which lack an experienced managerial class and which also lack investors who are willing and able to supply capital to industry. Incidentally, this means that Karl Marx was wrong — the development of capitalistic industry is not necessary in order to prepare a country for socialism. In fact, this development is likely to mean that the country never adopts socialism.

Government ownership and operation of industry may be widely extended in some countries by Socialist parties loyal to the traditional dogma, even though in those countries public ownership serves no economic purpose. In the United States, however, government ownership and operation of industry is likely to be confined to a few fields of industry where there are special reasons for it. Examples are industries that have trouble in making ends meet, such as urban transportation; industries that the people desire to have subsidized, such as housing or rural electrification; or industries that are inextricably connected with certain public purposes, such as electric power associated with navigation, flood control, or irrigation. But this special and limited expansion of public ownership is not socialism — much as some Socialists and some of their opponents would like to have us believe that it is.

The fact of the matter is that government ownership and operation of industry does not have the attraction for reformers that it had a generation or two ago. For this there are several reasons. One is that public ownership on an extensive scale is now a reality in a number of countries. Both its good points and its limitations have been revealed by experience. In the nineteenth century, socialism could be represented as the way of achieving a sort of Utopia. Today, widespread experience with government ownership and operation has robbed the socialist ideal of most of its glamour. Another reason why the socialist ideal has lost much of its appeal is a gradual awareness of the fact that the kind of administration and policy-making which democratic governments tend to develop are not the kind of administration and policy-making that suit industry. Democracies, as a rule, put into office cautious and conventional men whom the voters trust precisely because of these qualities. On the whole, this is as it should be. In times of crisis, it is true that the life of a democracy may depend upon bold and pioneering leadership. In ordinary times, however, decisions on major government policies should not be reached until public opinion has had time to understand the problem and the necessity for the proposed action. But a dynamic and progressive industry requires original, daring, and imaginative administration — precisely the kind that a democratic government is not well qualified to provide.[1]

Still another reason why government ownership and op-

[1] Dictators may have boldness and originality, but they do not tolerate these qualities in subordinates.

eration of industry has lost popular appeal is that the government has gained enormously in size and power, so that plenty of private enterprise is needed to keep a better distribution of power between government and industry. Time was when more government ownership of industry was urged for the very reason that it would give much-needed additional power to the government. The size and power of the government, however, have been growing rapidly — the Federal government has as many employees as nine General Motors Corporations would have, and the number of its employees (including government enterprises) has more than quadrupled in twenty years. Less power in the government and more in private hands would now improve the balance.

THE TWO TYPES OF PLANNED ECONOMY

Nor does a planned economy seem likely to develop. There are two types of planned economy: the budget type in which the government determines how much of each good is produced; and the nonbudget type in which the government exercises general control over the volume of incomes and of spending, and over the distribution of incomes, but leaves people free on the whole to produce and consume as they see fit.

A planned economy of the budget type is unlikely in the United States. It might work in a country where only a few kinds of goods were produced and where the demand for various kinds of goods was quite stable. But the task of making production plans for the multitude of industries in the United States would be extraordinarily formidable. And the task would be made far more difficult by rapid changes in technology, rapid shifts in demand, and the sudden growth of new kinds of demand. Finally, the difficulties of operating a planned economy of the budget type would be enormously increased by the policy of maintaining a high level of employment. This policy would leave only a small gap between the amount of low-cost productive capacity and the quantity of goods demanded in most industries. Consequently, if the production plans did not get goods made in the proportions demanded, there would be shortages that either would require rationing or would give rise to price increases. Planning of this type would be acceptable to the American people only if needed to meet a national emergency. It would not be acceptable as a normal way of operating the economy.

Nor is a planned economy of the second type likely to develop — one under which the government attempts to control the volume of money incomes for the purposes of maintaining a high level of employment, of keeping the economy stable, and of influencing the level of prices, and under which the government undertakes to control to some extent the distribution of income. The government will endeavor to do these things — or at least will pretend to do them — but should its efforts be called "planning"? The advocates of planning overlook the way in which democracies operate. There are often more or less serious differences over objectives, or at least over which objectives should be given preference, and there are usually differences over the best means for promoting any given objective.

In the field of economic policy there will undoubtedly be wide agreement over the desirability of maintaining a high level of employment and keeping production and employment stable. But agreement on the best ways to promote these objectives is not easily reached. Control of consumer credit, for example, helps to narrow fluctuations in expenditures for consumer goods and thus promotes stability of production and employment; but bankers, commercial credit companies, and many retailers do not believe that government control of the terms of consumer credit is necessary or desirable. Farmers urge that price or income supports for agriculture would make the economy more stable; but the levels at which farmers wish prices or incomes to be supported are far higher than much of the community regards as necessary. The pursuit of full employment, as I have pointed out, is likely to require a choice between the acceptance of a rising price level and some control over wages and prices. And attempts to strengthen the spirit of enterprise and to stimulate the growth of business come into conflict with attempts to limit differences in the size of personal incomes.

All of this means that, in a democracy such as ours, government intervention in economic affairs is bound to be a series of compromises. Some of the compromises are between people or groups who differ as to which of several objectives is more important; some are between people and groups who do not agree on what means will best promote certain objectives. The essential point is that such compromises are inherent in democracies; they are necessary to preserve the cohesiveness of the community and thus to make democratic processes work, but they are not planning. No general agreement on objectives and means is ever reached; no body of consistent and co-ordinated policies is ever developed. One policy, which meets the desires of part of the community, is adopted, and other policies which partly counteract the effects of the first policy and which meet the desires of other groups are also adopted.

All of which means that democracy and planning are to a considerable extent incompatible — they are compatible only to the extent that there is pretty general agreement about the relative importance of objectives and about the best ways of attaining these objectives. It is more important, of course, to have a democratic economy than a planned one.

How Much More Welfare?

Is a "welfare" economy likely to develop? A welfare economy may be defined as one which has regular arrangements for distributing an appreciable amount of income on the basis of need. Sometimes a means test is required; sometimes, as in the case of social insurance, income is given regardless of ability to pay. A distinction should be made between a "welfare economy" and a "handout economy." A handout economy is one in which the government payments or subsidies are made without careful regard for the importance of needs but for the purpose of buying votes.

A mixture of humanitarianism and vote-buying motives is inevitable, but the relative importance of the two motives may vary considerably. When the Congress orders the government to buy the entire silver output of the country at above-the-market prices or establishes such high supports for the prices of farm products that the government must purchase agricultural commodities in the midst of a boom, it is difficult to see humanitarian motives. There seems to be more humanitarianism in providing aid to dependent children who do not vote than in authorizing old-age assistance payments to elderly people who do vote.

The economy of the future will be more of a welfare economy than is the economy of today. Possibly it will also be more of a handout economy. At any rate the community, as I have pointed out in Chapters III and IV, has for some time gradually been demanding that the government assume more and more responsibility for seeing that important needs be met either out of public funds or through arrangements required by law. One of the first steps in the development of the welfare state was the establishment of free public education — strongly opposed at the time but now pretty generally taken for granted. Workmen's compensation laws, old-age assistance, unemployment compensation, old-age and survivors' insurance, and aid to the blind and to dependent children have followed.

The tendency to develop regular arrangements to provide income on the basis of need will continue. There will probably be a continuation of the tendency to discard the means test in determining whose needs shall be met and to set up insurance schemes that provide benefits regardless of the beneficiary's ability to meet his own needs. It would be desirable for the country to develop principles to guide the decision as to what needs should be met out of general revenues and what through special schemes. Undoubtedly, economists and political scientists in criticizing the decisions made will develop such principles. These principles could become important in determining what kind of needs the government meets and what kind it does not meet.

WHO WILL MAKE THE DECISIONS?

What will the economy of the United States during the next several decades be like? I do not think that it will lend itself to brief, neat description. It will be a mixture of different and, to some extent, conflicting principles. The intervention of the government in economic matters will be extensive. Special-interest groups, such as veterans, trade unions, old persons, farmers, and various business groups, will be numerous and well organized and will possess great influence. But in spite of the rise of government intervention in economic matters and the influence of special-interest groups, the most important characteristic of our economy will remain unchanged. That is the fact that decision-making will continue in the main to be decentralized. The most crucial decisions, the decisions as to what shall be made and what methods shall be used, will be made by millions of enterprises, and they will be guided by the decisions of more than a hundred million consumers.

What should this type of economy be called? The tremendous influence of employees suggests the term "laboristic economy"—though other special-interest groups possess much power. Another term is "mixed economy." Certainly the economy will be a mixed one, a mixture of direction by the government and by special-interest groups and of individual pursuit of self-interest. Unfortunately, the expression "mixed economy" gives no clue as to the ingredients in the mixture. J. M. Clark has termed the economy "decentralized collectivism." [2] This expression indicates the elements in the mixture, but gives the wrong impression as to their relative importance. The decentralized decision-making is more important than the central controls. One might use the term "regulated individualism," but this expression is awkward. The term "mixed economy" seems best to suggest that the economy represents several conflicting principles of control.

That the economy today represents a mixture of principles and that it will continue to do so is not surprising. A moment's reflection will reveal that a democratic and dynamic society is bound to have institutions that represent different and, quite possibly, conflicting principles. Each generation produces some institutions and policies of its own. The old institutions and policies are partly supplanted, but not entirely. It is freedom that permits these contradictions and conflicts in institutions and policies to arise. An orderly and efficient dictatorship would be less tolerant of inconsistencies and conflicts between old institutions and new. Where freedom and democracy flourish, one must expect the economy to be far from neat and orderly.

Let us look more closely at the way in which decisions will be made in the economy of the near future.

[2] *Alternative to Serfdom,* p. 121.

The role of the government in the economy. The growing role that the government may be expected to play was discussed in Chapter IV.

The influence of employees. The fact that four out of five workers in the United States are employees assures that the culture, laws, and institutions of America will be largely those of free employees, not those of self-employed, landowners, or any other form of property owners. The employee culture of America, however, will not be a proletarian culture or even a trade-union culture. Professional employees, supervisors, technicians, skilled craftsmen, and white-collar workers, together with the self-employed, make up half of the labor force of the country. Only about one fourth of the labor force are unskilled laborers, and this proportion is decreasing. A community made up almost entirely of employees will be inevitably more interested in the problems of employees than in the problems of property owners. It remains to be seen whether such a community can be persuaded that employees have an interest in a vigorous spirit of enterprise and whether it can be induced to give adequate incentives to pioneers and economic adventurers. The fact that the great majority of workers are employees means that trade unions will have great influence, particularly with respect to most matters that especially concern unions and employees. There appear to be some differences, however, between the views of trade union officers and the majority of employees on some proposals to regulate the activity of trade unions. Furthermore, as I have pointed out in Chapter IV, on many important issues, such as foreign policy, taxation, and agricultural policies, that do not concern them as employees, the employees as a whole, including members of unions, are very much divided. With respect to these issues the influence of unions will probably be quite limited.

The influence of business in the economy. By business is meant the self-employed (including the farmers) and the managements of corporations who usually represent the interests of stockholders. Up to now, as I have pointed out in Chapter III, the stockholders of corporations have been quite limited in number. They have consisted in the main of managerial and technical employees of corporations, professional people, and self-employed business owners. The influence of business will be far less than it possessed before 1929, but will probably be more (on most issues) than it possessed in 1950. This gain will be partly made possible by the increase which will probably occur in the number of stockholders. If the number of stockholders does not grow, business will have a harder time gaining influence. The rise in the number of stockholders will have to be accomplished largely by persuading employees to put part of their savings into stocks — let us hope into good issues, because otherwise the increase in the number of shareholders may bring corporations much ill will. This does not mean that employees should buy stock in the enterprises for which they work. In the case of nonexecutive employees, the fact that a man works for a concern is a good reason for his *not* buying stock in it. He diversifies his risks more satisfactorily if he invests in other concerns. Indeed, many employees can safely become stockholders only by investing in well-managed investment trusts. Employees who become

stockholders in American business will still have the point
of view, in the main, of employees rather than of business
owners. Nevertheless, in a community in which industry is
broadly owned, the problems of business owners are bound
to be better understood and to receive more sympathetic
treatment than in a community in which industry is nar-
rowly owned.

The gain in the influence of business will partly reflect
an improvement in the presentation of its point of view.
Until recent years the direct influence of business on public
policy was so great that business did not have to persuade
the public or public officials to accept its ideas. Now that
business must gain support by persuading people who are
not inclined to accept its views, it is having to learn how
to present its opinions. In 1950 business was doing an indifferent job of presenting its views and, in particular, was
presenting many conclusions that were not the result of
careful research and thought. Since there is much room for
improvement, the influence of business may be expected to
grow.

The influence of other organized groups. The farmers
have so many special interests that, although they should
be included in the business group for many purposes, they
should be regarded as a separate group for other purposes.
The influence of farmers upon public policies affecting agriculture will be great. The veterans and the aged will also
leave their mark on public policies — especially fiscal policies.

Some limitations on the influence of special groups.
The influence of all these special groups — trade unions,
business, the farmers, the aged, the veterans — and many

other smaller groups will be limited by the fact that the program of each group is narrow and selfish and consequently commands little support among nonmembers. The influence of the pressure groups will be limited also by their inability to develop influential leaders of thought. A certain disinterestedness of viewpoint, a deep concern for the welfare of the country as a whole, seems to be necessary for the production of important thinking. That seems to be the reason why the pressure groups have developed almost no great leaders of thought. American business, for example, has produced many great men of action, but only within the last decade or so has it begun to turn out important thinkers. Perhaps in the future the special-interest groups will have better success in developing important thinkers — men who are more than intellectual errand boys for their groups, who concern themselves with the problems of the country as well as the programs of their own groups but who apply in the analysis of general issues their intimate knowledge of the problems of their own group.

The influence of individual decision-making. The controversies of recent years over the intervention by the government in economic affairs and over the position of organized groups in the economy have tended to distract attention from the continued importance of individuals. Nevertheless, the economy of the United States is still predominantly run by the decisions of more than a hundred million individuals and of ten million business enterprises. Government economic policies enormously influence these decisions, but not always in the way that the government intends. Support for a price, for example, may simply stimulate the development of substitute commodities. Attempts to limit the output of a farm product by acreage control may increase the use of fertilizers. The government provides a framework within which individual decisions are made. Often the government encourages one type of decision and discourages other types. It is of particular importance, however, that ultimate decisions are made by individual consumers and by individual enterprises or producers.

Of special significance is the great opportunity that decentralized decision-making gives for experimentation and innovation. The pioneers who are responsible for technological progress are always a minority — often a minority of one. In the American economy a minority of one has a chance. The man who thinks that a new process will work or a new product will sell needs to persuade only one enterprise in an industry that his idea is worth trying out, and the idea or process will be tested. If it works, it will be imitated. Economies in which decision-making is highly centralized are at a serious disadvantage in competing with economies that have millions of centers of initiative.

The development of science, the spread of education, particularly high school and college education, the rise in incomes and of opportunities to travel, all tend to develop the kind of individuals who cannot be easily controlled — individuals who have their own ideas and their own reasons for their conclusions. It is primitive societies that are custombound, that produce conformists with few original thinkers or leaders. The more educated individuals become, the more inclined they are to do their own thinking. In a fundamental sense, society is not becoming less individualistic — it is becoming more so.

THE INFLUENCE OF IDEAS

The course of history is guided in large measure by ideas. A fruitful way of attempting to decide what future developments in the economy are probable is to ask what important changes in ideas are likely to occur in the second half of the twentieth century. What important ideas are declining in acceptance? What important new ideas are winning or are likely to win acceptance? How will changes in thinking affect economic policies and economic institutions?

Two principal ideas that have had a tremendous impact upon the course of history during the last hundred years are being discarded. Since ideas are an important part of the environment in which men live, the dropping of two influential ideas is a fact of great significance. One of these ideas is the view that the pursuit of individual self-interest can be relied upon to advance the interests of the community; the other is the Marxian view that human relations are explained by a struggle between economic classes and that history is essentially the story of the class struggle. Accompanying this view of history is the belief that the class struggle can be terminated and a sort of Utopia achieved by a revolution that will expropriate the owners of private property.

The idea that the pursuit of individual self-interest could be relied upon to promote the common interests of all members of the community led public policy in the last century to give greater freedom to individuals than ever before and helped to produce an extraordinarily rapid development of applied science. The idea that history is essentially a struggle between classes has been a powerful instrument of revolution. It has helped build up a religion of hatred among poverty-stricken millions and at the same time it has given them hope by convincing them that violent revolution will bring Utopia.

Some of the reasons for the abandonment of the idea that the common interests can be adequately promoted by giving people freedom to pursue their self-interest were discussed in Chapter I. But the reaction against the idea has gone too far and has caused the useful results of the pursuit of self-interest to be underestimated.[3] Less pronounced is revolt against the view that history is essentially a struggle between classes and that revolution will eventually end classes and the class struggle. Indeed, in Asia the view that history is merely a struggle between classes is still gaining adherents. In Western Europe, however, where the idea has never won more than limited acceptance, its influence is declining. It is apparent that the Marxian view of history is an oversimplified one, that history has been pretty much a mixture of conflict and co-operation, and that the conflicts have not always been economic ones.

What ideas are gaining in acceptance and are likely to be important in influencing economic history during the next generation or two? Any list of ideas that are growing in

[3] The fact that increases in profits are usually achieved only by giving buyers more for their money, so that the increase means gains for the buyers as well as for the sellers, is an example.

influence is almost certain to omit some that will turn
out to be of great significance. The following four, however, seem destined to have a major influence upon economic
institutions and policies during the next several decades.

1. *The idea that the government must be an instrument
of economic policy, intervening at many points in economic
matters.* The rise of this idea is associated with the decline
in the faith in the efficacy of laissez faire. It is now recognized that the way in which individuals and enterprises
pursue their interests depends upon the system of rights
and duties provided by the law, and that one of the responsibilities of government is to provide the system of rights and
duties that gives maximum scope to the pursuit of self-
interest by making pursuit of self-interest promote common
interests. But this means that the government is an instrument of economic policy.

2. *The idea that there are no panaceas, no cure-alls for
human ills, no sudden and complete solutions for problems.*
The rise of democracy and participation of the whole community in policy-making led for a time to some naïve and
highly optimistic thinking about the possibility of discover-
ing magical cures for economic ills. Socialism was proposed
as a panacea, so was Anarchism, the Single Tax, producers'
and consumers' co-operation, and various schemes for issu-
ing paper money. Experience with policy-making has made
the community increasingly skeptical of alleged cure-alls
and has taught people to think in terms of next steps and
of partial solutions for particular problems. Policy-making
has become less exciting but better informed and more
mature. This trend seems destined to continue.

3. *The idea that there must at all times be opportunity for all would-be workers to find employment, and that if there are not sufficient opportunities, the community should do something about this lack.* Like many important ideas, this one is not sharply defined and is not accompanied by answers to the many questions that it raises. The most obvious question is: "On what terms should jobs be available?" Perhaps the community will never have to face squarely that difficult question. The increasingly accepted view that large-scale chronic unemployment is intolerable may have far-reaching effects upon the scope and nature of government activities. Ample employment opportunities require that there be ample investment opportunities, but a society composed mainly of employees will be less interested in investment opportunities than in employment opportunities.

4. *The idea that the good life is something to be enjoyed here and now and that the community has the responsibility of seeing that all its members, regardless of economic status or race, have a fair chance at the good life.* This idea is an extension of the idea that there must always be ample employment opportunities — or perhaps it would be more accurate to say that the idea that there must always be enough jobs is simply a part of the idea that all members of the community must have a fair chance at the good life. That all persons must have a fair chance at the good life is simply another way of saying that the economy will be a welfare economy — or at least a mixture of a welfare and a handout economy. The present age has gone farther than any previous one in insisting that educational opportunities be given to men of all classes, that economic and social

barriers to opportunity be broken down, that men be given some minimum protection against the principal economic hazards. Present trends indicate that the community will go even farther in bringing opportunity and security to all of its members.

How Important Are the Economic Institutions of the United States?

How distinctive and important are the economic and political institutions of the United States? Are these institutions merely the most productive that men have ever developed, or do they possess more important values? Do they possess important political and moral superiorities that should make men cherish them and hence, if necessary, fight for them?

The answer to the last two questions is "Yes." There are two principal reasons for this answer. One reason is that American economic institutions produce a fairly well-balanced division of power — an important political advantage. The other reason is that American institutions give extraordinary opportunities to the individual and also place enormous responsibilities upon him.

Power in the American community is pretty well divided between the government, corporate executives, farmers, organized small business, and trade unions. Furthermore, the power of all kinds of organizations, especially the government, is limited by the wide scope of individual decision-making. The division of power is not perfect. The great lack is effective representation of the consumer interests, and there is no immediate prospect that this lack will be remedied. But the wide scope of individual decision-making helps compensate for the absence of organized representation of consumer interests. Among the organizations themselves the power of each is limited by the other organizations. The government is held in check by the corporations, the organized small businessmen, the farmers, and the unions; the corporations by the government, organized small business, the unions, and, in some industries, by the farmers; the small businessmen by the government, the unions, and the corporations; and the unions by the government, the corporations, the farmers, and small business.

One may ask just what kind of interest is meant by "the government" and question whether it should really be considered a separate source of power. In a democracy must not the men who make, interpret, and administer laws reflect public opinion and, to that extent, are they really an independent source of power comparable to businessmen, farmers, trade unionists, or consumers? Are they not simply instruments through which various interests in the community express themselves?

It is true that public officials reflect public opinion and that they do not as a rule act until public opinion has developed to a certain point. This does not mean, however, that public officials are mere rubber stamps and do not play a creative role in guiding the development of public opinion or in selecting policies. Public opinion is usually pretty much divided. Consequently, public officials are likely to be the originators of compromises — compromises that do not fully reflect the view of any group but stand a chance of commanding a majority. Obviously the formulation of compromises offers great opportunity for creativeness. On many important issues the public is so poorly informed and public opinion is so incompletely developed that government officials have a wide range of discretion in proposing policies. Furthermore, they have considerable discretion in administering policies and in interpreting laws. They also have the authority and resources to make all manner of investigations and thus to determine in considerable measure what facts are known about the economy and how they are brought to the attention of the public.

It seems clear that the holders of both elective and appointive offices represent a separate source of power in the community. The power of elected officers comes ultimately from their ability to command enough votes to win elections, and the power of the appointive officers comes either through their ability to win the confidence of elected officers or from the fact that they hold their offices for life or for long terms. The support of organized groups is often important in helping men win elections, but the point of view of most elected officers is different from the separate viewpoints of the groups from which their support comes.

The most valuable characteristic of the American economy is the opportunity and the responsibility that it gives to the individual. This is a result of the decentralization of decision-making. One of the underlying trends in the development of civilization has been the tendency to raise the importance of individuals relative to institutions. In primitive societies individuals are quite completely subordinated to the discipline of the group. This discipline does not encourage individuals to be nonconformists or protect them when they are. It does not encourage them to think new thoughts, to use new methods, to make new products, or to break away from established modes of living. The process of civilization consists in a reversal of the relationship between individuals and institutions. Instead of the individual's being subordinated to institutions, institutions become the means to help individuals more completely in achieving the good life.

Many people fear that the growth of government intervention in economic matters and the rise of many organized groups mean that the long-established tendency to free individuals from the domination of institutions is being reversed and that the individual initiative, independence, and resourcefulness are insidiously being sapped by the slow transfer of decision-making to organizations. History shows that every now and then men become so much dominated by their institutions that a reformation or revolt is necessary to weaken the grip of institutions on individuals. During the next several decades, the transfer of decision-making to the government and to other organizations may go so far that it will ultimately provoke a reaction in favor of more decision-making by individuals.

There is no convincing evidence, however, in the United States at least, that the widening activities of the government and of other organizations represent a reversal of the centuries-old trend toward individual emancipation. The distinguishing characteristic of the economy will continue to be the large scope that it offers for individuals to be themselves, to make their own decisions, to make their living as they see fit. That, incidentally, is the essence of the case that the American economy offers against Communism. For what does Communism offer the individual? Simply the opportunity to be a cog in a vast machine, to do what he is told to do in the way that he is told to do it, to conform, to be an efficient part of the larger whole, to behave according to plan.

Opportunity for individuals also means responsibility. An economy in which there is great individual initiative will be dynamic and progressive — and, as I have implied earlier in this chapter, messy. It will be a jumble of institutions and policies that are imperfectly co-ordinated and, to some extent, inconsistent. Such an economy will have plenty of problems. In fact, *any* dynamic and progressive economy is bound to have problems — and the more dynamic and progressive it is, the more problems it will have. Problems are situations to which traditional rules of conduct do not apply and for which new rules of conduct must be developed. Such problems are solved by "progress" or change, but the fund of unsolved problems is also increased by progress. That is why dynamic economies have more problems than stagnant societies. Undoubtedly the problems of our economy will continue to worry many people and to cause them to look on the future of mankind as dark — just as do the problems of today. One of many possible samples of this prevalent viewpoint is the assertion of Aldous Huxley that "the nations of the West are all sick societies disintegrating under the impact of an advancing technology."

But problems that stem from rapid changes in technology and in ways of making a living are on the whole good for the community, provided they are not too numerous. Unsolved problems tend to divide a community, because there are differences of opinion over how those problems should be solved; and there is a limit to the number and seriousness of the differences that a community can have and still be a community. On the other hand, new problems have the important advantage of compelling the community to be morally creative — to extend and modify its ethical system to fit new conditions. The process of adapting the ethical system to new conditions will often be stormy and will undoubtedly produce many self-seeking arguments. Disagreements over what is fair or right may produce, for the time being at least, a sort of moral chaos — but it will be a healthy kind of chaos. It will not mean that people are indifferent to right and wrong; on the contrary, it will mean that they are keenly interested in the rules that govern conduct, that they are searching for better rules, and that they are willing to support their positions vigorously. By forcing the members of the community constantly to improve and extend its ethical codes, a dynamic economy gives dignity and significance to the lives of millions of men.

Index

Index